The Chippewas of Georgina Island

Also by John Steckley from Rock's Mills Press

Gibbons: The Invisible Apes
Parrots: The Flock Among Us
The Memoirs of Alexander Brodie (editor)
The Names of the Wyandot
Stories for Mia
Sophia B. Jones: The First Canadian Black Woman to Become a Doctor

The Chippewas of Georgina Island
A People of Stories

John Steckley

Rock's Mills Press
Rock's Mills, Ontario • Oakville, Ontario
2025

Published by
Rock's Mills Press
www.rocksmillspress.com

Copyright © 2025 by John Steckley.
All rights reserved. Reproduction in whole or in part without the written permission of the publisher is strictly prohibited.

This is a work of fiction. Names, characters, places and incidents either are products of the author's imagination or are used fictitiously. Any resemblance to actual events or locales or persons, living or dead, is entirely coincidental.

Library and Archives Canada Cataloguing in Publication data has been applied for by the publisher.

Rock's Mills Press is a registered trademark used under license.

For information, including bulk, retail and wholesale orders and permissions requests, please contact the Publisher at customer.service@rocksmillspress.com.

Contents

CHAPTER ONE
Introduction | 1

CHAPTER TWO
Stories of Snake Island | 8

CHAPTER THREE
The People Develop Their Agriculture | 30

CHAPTER FOUR
Charles Big Canoe Tells a Story | 39

CHAPTER FIVE
Going to School | 52

CHAPTER SIX
Black Ash Baskets, Fancy Work , and Woodwork | 67

CHAPTER SEVEN
Going Fishing | 75

CHAPTER EIGHT
Going to War | 86

CHAPTER NINE
The Crossing: The Challenge of Living on an Island | 100

CHAPTER TEN
Growing Up on Georgina Island in the Not-Too-Distant Past | 116

CHAPTER ELEVEN
Medicines and Medicine People | 135

CHAPTER TWELVE
Georgina Island Today | 143

Bibliography | 149

Acknowledgements

While many Chippewas of Georgina Island from a long line of generations have provided me with an outstanding amount of information for this book, I would like to acknowledge those who have taught me in person. My first contact was with Shelley Charles, a colleague of mine at Humber College, who asked me to put this book together. Elder Susan Hoeg and her daughter Lauri Hoeg taught me in person much of what I needed to know about the people. Their knowledge helped give me direction. I learned much about the language from Elder Barbara McDonald. Then there was Leah Atkinson, whose hospitality gave my wife and me a place to stay when we went to Georgina Island, and guided us through the community. Then there is my wife Angelika, who helped me in many ways to make this the book it became.

CHAPTER ONE

Introduction

A people's true character comes out in its stories. As American Indigenous author Thomas King famously wrote: "Stories are all that we are" (King, 2003). In this book, you will be given the opportunity to read some of the stories that demonstrate the strength of character and ability to survive and flourish of the Chippewas of Georgina Island. The individuals telling the tales in this book were born in the 18th, 19th and 20th centuries, and the characteristics they bear are very similar. Their descendants born in the 21st century will inherit these stories and add to them their own significant tales. Some of the stories are told with the many photographs contained in the book. These pictures often speak where the words have been lost.

The ancestors of the Chippewas of Georgina Island have been in the territory of Turtle Island (the Americas) for thousands of years. Especially early ancestors were on Turtle Island when the land known now as the province of Ontario was still covered by a glacier. Exactly when they came to live in Ontario is not known, but it is, again, thousands of years ago. There is a story that tells of their arrival from an earlier place.

Edward or Eddie Benton-Banai (1931–2020) is a greatly respected Anishinaabe Elder of the Lac Courte Oreilles Reservation in Wisconsin. He was a co-founder of the American Indian Movement. He set in print many of the traditions of the people in his influential *The Mishomis Book: The Voice of the Ojibway* (Benton-Banai, 1988). The word *mishomis* means 'grandfather.' In the chapter entitled "The Migration of the Anishinaabe," he writes of a time when his people, and related peoples such as the Abenaki that speak Algonquian languages, lived along the coast of the Atlantic Ocean. A pregnant woman had a dream vision of standing on the back of a turtle that faced west. When discussed by the elders, it was felt that this was a vision of the island that had been foretold as the first of seven stopping places that their people would need to take to find a good place to live. This first place is thought by many to be an island near present-day Montreal. Other stopping places included Niagara Falls, Manitoulin Island and present-day Sault Ste. Marie. Certain groups stayed along the way, and others moved on to Wisconsin (Benton-Banai, 1988, pp. 94–102).

The people call themselves Anishinaabe, as do other First Nations known as Chippewa and those otherwise known as Algonquin ('they are our relatives'[1]), Mississauga ('large river mouth'), Nipissing ('place of the elms'[2]), Odawa or Ottawa (based on the verb 'to trade'[3]), and Ojibwa. The name '*Anishinaabe*' (plural *Anishinaabek*) is usually translated as 'Original Man.' The 'naabe' part has a basic meaning of 'male' as used not only for humans, but for the males of animals as well (Baraga, 1992, p. 262). Still, the whole word refers to all Anishinaabe individuals, the people generally.

The names 'Chippewa' and 'Ojibwa' do not come from Anishinaabemowin (the language of the Anishinaabe people). They come from other Indigenous First Nations and are usually translated as 'puckered moccasins.' It is unfortunate but true that a large number of the names traditionally used to refer to the Indigenous people of Canada did not come from their language but from Europeans and from other Indigenous peoples (especially Cree). This outsider naming includes the names Assiniboine, Carrier, Cree, Dogrib, Eskimo, Huron, Iroquois, Mohawk, Seneca, Sioux and Slavey.

If you are greeted by someone from Georgina Island, you may be met with one of two words. One is 'ahneen' ('hello'). The other word is 'boozhoo'. There are two different stories about the origin of this word. It is easy to imagine it as a way of saying the French "bonjour," there being no -r- in the Anishinaabe language at the time of early contact. However, there is another story which needs to be heard. The culture hero of the Anishinaabe people is Nanabush,[4] a name sometimes pronounced as Nanaboozhoo. He was a mythic figure who altered the world and, likewise, was a trickster. It is said in some Anishinaabe stories that Nanabush said that he would return but would not say what form he would come back in.

When someone new came into the area, some people would ask a question, something like "Giin inna Nanaboozhoo," meaning "Are you Nanaboozhoo?" French traders hearing this could easily believe that the

---

1. This is generally said to come from the Algonquian language of the Malecite, who live in Quebec, New Brunswick and Maine.
2. The Nipissing live along the shores of Lake Nipissing in northern Ontario.
3. The Odawa live in Ontario, Michigan and Oklahoma.
4. According to renowned Anishinaabe Elder, linguist and author, Basil Johnston, the name is derived from a word meaning 'foolish' (Fleming, 2017).

Anishinaabe were saying 'hello' to them in greeting. Whatever the history of the word, it became a term of mutual friendly greeting between French and Anishinaabe, which the Chippewas of Georgina Island continue to this day.

Speaking of Nanabush, if you come to visit Georgina Island, you are encouraged to take a tour on what they call the nana bush trails. It is worth the walk.

In 1969, Chief Lorenzo Big Canoe[5] used the medium of a newspaper interview to tell a Nanabush story known as the Shut Eye Dance:

Hunting was scarce. Nanabush could not find game to fill his empty stomach, so he devised a plan. He built a big bark lodge at the centre of which was a fireplace. He was able to to talk to the birds and animals so he let it be known that he was holding a big dance for the birds and invited all to come out at a certain time.

After they had all assembled he told them they must dance while he sat, changed and beat his tom tom, but they must dance with their eyes closed. When he told them they must dance [in a] circle, he grabbed a nice fat duck or goose and tossed it behind him.

One little bird dared to peek and he saw what was happening, so he gave the alarm and headed for the doorway. Nanabush sprang up and as the bird was going out the door, gave him a swift kick, knocking all his tailfeathers out, and yelled that forever after he would have red eyes. That is why the little hell divers have red eyes and no tail. (Big Canoe, *Newmarket Era and Express*, February 11, 1969, p. 8)

Throughout this book, there will be stories told by Georgina Island people about the history and current life of the Georgina Islanders. Some of these stories were recorded in *The Georgina Island Storytelling Project* of 2006. The ones recorded in our manuscript are those that were written down. If you go to the website, there are stories that you can hear rather than read. They are well worth watching and hearing.

One such storyteller is Elder Susan Hoeg (née Vernon), who will be often quoted in this book. One of her stories is entitled *History of Georgina Island*, accompanied by the picture below. It presents an informative and lively picture introduction to that history.

---

5. The common Georgina surname 'Big Canoe' is written in Anishinaabemowin as *Keche* (big) *Chemon* (canoe).

Her accomplishments are not limited to her gift of telling stories. In 2009, she was awarded the Order of Ontario, which was primarily for the work that she did in helping First Nations women obtain Indian status after Bill C-31. That status had been taken away from them for marrying non-status men. Men did not lose their status by marrying non-status women. She wrote the following:

> Life on Georgina Island began in the early 1800s. The Department of Upper Canada wanted to separate the Indians from the white settlements, and putting them on reservations was a way of accomplishing this.
>
> After a nomadic way of life, they found it difficult to stay in one area. In 1826, camp meetings were held by the Methodist missionaries who worked vigorously to convert Indians to Christianity. Schooling was encouraged, and children were placed with mission families. They were trained to spread the Christian faith and were forbidden to practice their Native Teachings or to use their Native tongue. Boarding schools were to follow, taking children away from heartbroken families.
>
> In the late 1820s, the Indian Department of Upper Canada began to relocate the Lake Simcoe Indians. The Indians were blamed for destroying wildlife, so they were encouraged to farm.
>
> Snake Island was the first island the Indians settled on in Lake Simcoe. With more pressure to farm, they moved to the larger and

more isolated Georgina Island. Only a few remained on Snake Island. The population on Georgina Island in 1876 was 131. They gradually changed their lifestyles, making the island their home.

About 1900, my grandfather built our log house. This is the warm, loving home I spent my childhood in. My grandfather always won a prize for the best garden. Strawberries, raspberries and a variety of vegetables ensured enough food for the hard winters.

He rowed across the lake in a boat he had built. Every week, the supplies were shopped for in the nearby towns. Hours were spent carving axe handles while my grandmother made beautiful baskets trimmed with sweet grass and porcupine quills. They would then take them to the villages and sell or trade them for food or clothes.

In the spring, maple syrup boiled vigorously in big black pots. Medicines were gathered in the woods. The women nursed the sick and delivered the babies.

We had an Indian Agent who looked after the affairs of our people. He always frightened me. Our men and women fought in the wars, some never returned. In 1961, the Native people were finally able to vote in the federal elections. They were also then allowed to bring alcohol onto the reserves. In the early 1950s, the telephone was brought to the island by underwater cable, and then hydro arrived in 1959.

Today, we enjoy a new ferryboat and hovercraft. Our revenues come from leased land on Fox, Snake and Georgina Island. We have an elected Chief and four councillors. Our island membership is 600, and 155 members reside in our reserve. We enjoy a new Community Centre, Health Centre, United Church and a Public School. Classes are taught in Native language, art beadwork and traditional teachings. We have a ball team and a hockey team; we enjoy Powwows and Native dancing.

Self-government is in the future. Our way of life is changing; we hope and pray it's for the better.

Moving South to Lake Simcoe

For centuries, the people who came to make Georgina Island their home lived on or near the north shore of Lake Huron. That would change in the mid-17th century. During that time, the Haudenosaunee (whom the French called the 'Iroquois') drove the Wendat (whom the French called the 'Huron') from their territory and moved into the rich lands of south-central Ontario.

The Haudenosaunee did not stay there long. During the 1690s, Anishinaabe travelled from the area north of Lake Superior and Lake Huron to move into southern Ontario, including the Lake Simcoe region, but extending directly south as well, along the Holland River. They had to fight their way there, driving out the Mohawk and other Haudenosaunee nations from their newly acquired territory. Although stories of this fight are not often recorded in history books, the people have long carried tales of that time of moving and struggle in Anishinaabe communities throughout Ontario. The Anishinaabe place name *Nottawasaga,* referring to the river mouth and the river of that name, means 'the river mouth of the snake' (meaning the Haudenosaunee, and not in the respectful way that relates to the last name 'Snake'), signifying the place where that people were waiting to fight the Anishinaabe. There is an island, Bone Island (formerly known as Skull Island), northeast of Beausoleil Island, whose name was said to come from the pile of Haudenosaunee skulls once found there (Schmalz, 1991, p. 24).

Another story still told speaks of that time as well. Serious fighting took place between the two peoples along the shores of Lake Simcoe, notably near what is now the city of Orillia. On Georgina Island today, there is a tale still spoken of a tree known as 'bone-hang' that grows on the eastern part of the island. According to the centuries-old story, the bone that hangs in the tree is of a Haudenosaunee warrior killed during one of the many battles between the two peoples during the seventeenth century. Not all storytellers agree as to the nature of this particular bone. One Elder told me that he thinks that the bone came from a cow. No matter who or what the original owner of the bone was, tales of the ancient battles persist.

In 1763, after the defeat of the French by the British, an important document for Indigenous land rights in what are now the eastern provinces was signed, called the Royal Proclamation. It stated that the only way that land could be taken from First Nations people was by "public purchase," that is, by treaty.

On May 22, 1798, five leaders of the people that included the ancestors of the Chippewas of Georgina Island signed Treaty #5 or the Penetanguishene Purchase, which involved a transfer of the land from Nottawasaga Bay facing the southern shore of Georgian Bay east to include all of the Penetang Peninsula. For this valuable property, the people received £101.[6]

Closer to their eventual home was the next big treaty, which was negotiated shortly after the Chippewas had fought alongside the British and Canadians in the War of 1812. It was known as Lake Simcoe Treaty #16, signed on November 17 and 18, 1815. The ones inking the agreement were the leaders of the three different bands in the area, including Kinaybicoinini[7] ('Snake Man') or Joseph Snake, who was the earliest recorded chief of the people who would become known as the Chippewas of Georgina Island. The land surrenders comprised 250,000 acres (over 1,000 square kilometres) between Kempenfelt Bay on the north of Lake Simcoe and Lake Huron. For this vast tract of land, the people received only £4,000 (less than $8,000 in today's money), a little over £60 (less than $120) an acre.

On October 17, 1818, the people were one of the bands involved with a huge surrender (1,592,000 acres) of their territory, including land important to the band, south of Kempenfelt Bay, the western shore of Lake Simcoe, and from Cook's Bay at the south of the lake down through Holland River. All of the bands involved would collectively receive the sum of £1,200 annually.

In the 1830s, the people were forced together with closely related peoples to move to a single piece of land in the Orillia area that was planned by the government of the time to be a great 'civilization' project. Although the people did their best to adapt to this imposed move and lumping together, the Chippewas of Georgina Island were within a few years forced to move back, to Snake Island, and then Georgina Island.

---

6. On February 18, 2024, the British pound was worth $1.70 Canadian.
7. The part meaning 'snake' is 'kindybico' and 'inini' means 'male'.

Chapter Two

Stories of Snake Island

Before the people made their home on Georgina Island, they lived a little farther west by the southwest corner of Lake Simcoe, on the smaller island named Snake Island.

The first written Indigenous place name that appears for Snake Island is the Wendat (Huron) *Ondioe*, which means 'at the place where a point of land is in water,' probably referring to the shallow water that separated the island from the mainland at that time. This name was written down in the 17th century, when the Wendat lived in the area and used the island for temporary hunting and fishing.

The Wendat called Lake Simcoe *Wentaronk*, meaning 'poles that cross', referring to the fish weirs made of large, long cedar poles that crossed the fast-flowing waters of the Atherley Narrows between Lake Simcoe and Lake Couchiching (a name based on the Anishinaabemowin word 'gojijing' 'at the inlet') in what is now the town of Orillia. Archaeologists have dated the first such poles being erected as long as 4,500 years ago. The fish could not easily swim past the poles, making it a great place to spear fish. These same poles give the name *Mnjikaning* ('at the fish fence') to the area and to the Anishinaabe community (long known by the non-Indigenous name 'Rama') that is situated there today. The Mohawk,[8] in their short period in the area after driving off the Wendat, would call it *Tkaronto* (later converted to *Toronto*), meaning, like the related Wendat term, 'trees or poles in water', referring to the same fish weir.

In the 1780s Chief Joseph Snake (*Ginibeganini*, literally 'Snake man'), a man possibly then in his forties, and his band moved into the area of Snake Island (named after him). It is one of three islands, including Georgina and Fox Island, which had not been surrendered to the British Crown. It is important to note that in the 19th century the people did not restrict

---

8. The name 'Mohawk' was given to them by their Algonquian neighbours in the northeastern U.S. It means 'man eaters'. Their own term for themselves is Kanyenkehaka 'people of the flint'.

themselves to just living on and using the islands. Their territory included surrounding areas on the mainland, in particular the area south and west of Lake Simcoe. In an article he wrote for the *Newmarket Era and Express*, published on February 11, 1960, Chief Lorenzo Big Canoe, a great-great-grandson of Joseph Snake, explains:

> Chief Snake and his followers took a course that brought them along the west shore of Lake Simcoe and camped at various locations along the way, living for quite some time at the mouth of the Holland River [Cook's Bay, Lake Simcoe] and Bradford, later settling on Snake Island. (Big Canoe, 1960)

The people's connection to parts of the Holland River, including the Holland Landing area, for a while the northern limit of Yonge Street and the location of a trading post/depot run by the North West Company, has never been completely, formally recognized. This was despite the fact that Chief John E. Big Canoe spoke during the Williams Treaties negotiations of 1923 of his grandfather and great-uncle as having rights to two branches of the Holland River south of Lake Simcoe, and other Georgina Island band members spoke of hunting rights there being reserved for their use by Lieutenant-Governor John Simcoe (Blair, 2008, pp. 131–2).

There were two temporary camps there where people would stay when hunting, fishing and trading in the area. Stories are told of people being buried there in graves that are unmarked and still unrecognized. It is certainly hoped that they will be found someday.

There were three Anishinaabe bands that moved down into the area. Chief Joseph Snake led the one that travelled the furthest south. Chief John Assance[9] ('Little Clam or Shell'), leader of the Otter clan, headed another, which would become the Beausoleil/Christian Island band of southern Georgian Bay. Then there was the Mnjikaning/Rama band led by Chief Yellowhead.

The story of the extended territory and the long fight that the people had to maintain their rights to that territory will be told in the discussion of the Williams Treaties.

Chief Joseph Snake was the last chief for life of the people, and his life was a long one, extending well into his nineties. After him there were regular

---

9. To learn more about John Assance, read Hall, 2003.

elections for chief, and then chief and council. In his time, and still today, there is a great significance to clans or totems among the people. The word *totem* itself comes from *Anishinaabemowin*.[10] It is derived from the word *ndodem* (or ntotem) meaning 'my clan', the root word for clan being *-ote-*. As Lorenzo Big Canoe would write in 1960:

> It is only about five generations since our people started using surnames. We did have a sign or totem pole system by which the children of a family took the totem of the father. In my own family our totem is the Otter and all my children belong to the Otter Clan. This system was intertribal as there are Indians from reserves north of here with the Otter totem who are definitely blood relatives. (Big Canoe, 1960)

There are on record speeches given by Joseph Snake and his fellow chief John Assance. Their people had not been treated by the government in a way that lived up to the fine speeches made years earlier by Governor John Graves Simcoe, so they came to state their case to a Major Smith at York (named later 'Toronto') on November 25, 1796. Relationships were tense between the Anishinaabe of the area around York and the Canadian soldiers. A Queen's Ranger (a member of a regiment that had been raised by Simcoe) had earlier that year killed a Mississauga chief, Wabakinine,[11] who was merely trying to protect his sister from sexual assault by a Queen's Ranger in the Mississauga encampment in York. No punishment for the man appeared to be forthcoming.

The two chiefs expressed their concern about the nature of the relationship between the two peoples.

A Speech from Keuebego Onene [Joseph Snake] and Escence [John Assance], two Indian chiefs from Lake Simcoe to Major Smith commanding at York 25 November 1796.

Father Our Great Father Governor Simcoe before he went away

---

10. It is not the only word in English that is derived from an Anishinaabemowin word. This is also true for 'muskeg' meaning 'grassy bog', muskellunge, which sometimes is given as meaning 'large fish', and 'chipmunk' which refers to 'facing downwards', the way you often see a chipmunk climbing down a tree.
11. For a description of his life and death, see Smith, 1979.

told us before several of you green coated Officers [i.e., the Queen's Rangers], that he was going over to the Great Lake, where His Father and our Great Father the King was, and in his absence the Council fire would be kept alive by you, and that whenever we had anything to say to our Father, we should come to this fire, and that we should be assisted in our distresses— You the Wolf interpreted this to us.

Father, several Indians in want of a little Tobacco have been refused. We are in want of some also. You say you have none. When our Father Governor Simcoe was with us, he was good to us. But now we are neglected. Yesterday we came here and sat at your doors; Not one of you would look at us

Father, I am sorry we are thrown away. And that our Great Father Governor Simcoe should have a sweet mouth, we are very thankful for the Provision you gave us— That is all we have to say. (Cruikshank and Hunter, 1932, p. 98)

The people participated on the British/Canadian side of the War of 1812. Ancestors of the people of Georgina Island and other Anishinaabe fighters significantly helped to defend the land their ancestors had lived in for so long (see the chapter "Going to War").

During the period 1815–18, along with the other two communities, the people were pressured into selling almost two million acres of land. Chief Joseph Snake and his people wisely ensured that the three islands of Snake Island, Georgina Island and Fox Island would remain in their possession.

In 1828 a good number of the members of the community had been converted to Christianity by Methodist missionaries, including some fellow Anishinaabe preachers.[12] By 1829, there were two mission buildings on the island, one for the mission school, and the other used for meetings. Remnants of the foundations of these two buildings still could be seen on Snake Island in the middle of the 20th century.

The Coldwater-Narrows Reserve

The band led by Chief Joseph Snake was comfortably settled on Snake Island when they were strongly pressured by the government under

---

12. See Smith, 1985, for the life story of Peter Jones (1802–1856), an influential Anishinaabe minister in southern Ontario at that time.

Lieutenant-Governor John Colborne to relocate to the Coldwater-Narrows reserve in 1830, the former name a translation of the Anishinaabe word Gisssinausebing, 'at the cold river'. This was comprised of some 9,800 acres in two large blocks of land 14 miles long, following an old portage route between the present towns of Orillia and Coldwater. All three local bands were moved there, amounting to around 500 people. The Mnjikaning band was led by Yellowhead's son William Yellowhead or Musquakie ('red earth', after whom some say Muskoka was named). They spent their money earned by the land sale on the building of houses and other necessities, and started farming the land. Within a year they had grown some 500 bushels of grain, and paid a substantial sum (around £800) to have a grist mill constructed in 1833–4 to grind their grain into flour. They were working hard to make the community a success, making the best of a situation into which that they had been forced.

The government did not show the same degree of dedication to the project, reducing its monetary support (which included money held 'in trust' for the people). This was especially the case when the administration of new Lieutenant-Governor Francis Bond Head took over in 1836. The people were forced to surrender their land through treaty, selling it to the government in that year. The money so earned would not be freely used by them, but would be held with a tight fist in trust by the government. By 1839, Chief Snake's band began to return to Snake Island. By 1842, there were 109 people living there.

Proper settlement payments for the loss of the land of the Coldwater project have only recently (2012) been arranged with the communities affected.

In 1850, George Copway or *Kahgegagahhowh* ('Standing Firm' or 'He who stands Forever'), an Anishinaabe from the Rice Lake area (east and a little south of Lake Simcoe), was the first Indigenous Canadian to write a best-selling book, *The Traditional History and Characteristic Sketches of the Ojibway Nation*. In that book he said this about the people of Snake Island:

> In 1842 they occupied one of the three Islands on Lake Simcoe, which have been set apart for the tribe many years previous. They were over one hundred in number and occupied twelve dwelling-houses. They had other buildings, and a school-house. The children were instructed

by a respectable teacher, and divine service was conducted by a resident missionary of the Methodist persuasion. They had about one hundred and fifty acres under cultivation, and were rapidly improving in habits of industry and agricultural skill.

Their missionary, who had been acquainted with them for about three years, stated that the majority of them were strictly moral in their character, —that most of the adults were decidedly pious, and that many of them, for consistency of character, would not suffer by comparison with white Christians of any denomination. (Copway, 1972, pp. 192–3)

The 1845 Census of Snake Island

The following is a census of the people in 1845. Some of the surnames still survive on Georgina Island today: As(h)quabe, Big Canoe, Blackbird, Charles, Johnson, Port(e) and York(e). People named Shilling and Simcoe are still found in the Chippewas of Rama (Mnjikaning) First Nation. Other family names have since disappeared from Georgina Island, but those bearing those names probably left descendants alive today on the island.

Ann, daughter of Chief Joseph Snake

Sept. 30th 1845 Numbers of Snake Island Tribe of Indians

6[13]*James York   3 Peter York
5 John Windigo   7 John Esquabe [Ashquabe]
4 John Simcoe   3 William Port
5 Paul Bigcanoe   6 Jacob Charles
5 Benjamin Crane   5 John Blackbird Senior
7 John Miller   2 John Blackbird Junior
7 John Snake   1 Mrs. Gremore*
3 John Beatty   3 Mrs. Bowland

---

13. The numbers represent how many family members there were. The use of * indicates a spelling or a number that is unclear in the original text.

3 David Snake   1 Anna Bowland
5 Joseph Snake Junior   1 Widow Beatty
4 Peter Kesagooh*   1 Mrs Canderrow*
3 Chief Joseph Snake   4 Eliza York
3 Thomas Bigsail   1 Widow Windigo
6 James Snake

The Blackbirds: A Snake Island and Georgina Island Family

You will see the name Blackbird mentioned several times in this book, as befits one of the long-term families in the community. The name is also found in a number of other Anishinaabe communities. John Blackbird, Jr., born circa 1811 in Orillia (i.e., Mnjiganing or Rama) moved to Snake Island, possibly with his father. His wife Catherine was born in 1814 in Orillia as well, and also moved to Snake Island.

Above left: Annie, Jim and Gertie Blackbird. Above right: Blackbird family. Below: Blackbird family with Mrs. Blackbird.

Chief Joseph Snake Speaks to Keep Possession of the Islands

In 1846, the government of Upper Canada was for its own administrative purposes pushing for the smaller bands to be joined into large communities and for the children of the Aboriginal communities to enroll in an early form of residential school. This was the yet-to-be-established Manual Labour School at Alnwick, on the land of the Alderville First Nation, by the shores of Rice Lake. On July 30 and 31 of that year, the leaders of the First Nations of southern Ontario met with the government officials. The purpose of the meeting was to gauge the Aboriginal response to the "Proposed Removal of the Smaller Communities and the Establishment of the Manual Labour Schools." Representing the Snake Island people were Chief Joseph Snake, his translator/orator or speaker John Snake, and Thomas Shilling, son of one of the chiefs of Rama, but resident on Snake Island. We have on record two short speeches spoken by John Snake, but stemming from the chief's ideas. In these speeches you can see that the words of Joseph and John Snake were eloquent, reflecting the ideas of a chief who democratically represented the wishes of his people, and who was not easily fooled by legalistic government rhetoric. He had heard many government promises, and knew not to trust them. Here we will present the first such speech, as it related to moving smaller bands into larger communities:

My Chiefs— You will now hear what I have to say; through my Orator.

The Orator, Mr. John Snake, stands by the Chief, then spoke as follows:

Fathers— You wish to hear the sentiments of the Indians, with regard to the speech sent by our Great Father. We have reflected on the subject, and I am now prepared to give an answer with regard to the wishes of our Great Father, or the future prosperity of the Indians. With regard to forming large settlements, I do not see any reasonable obstacle, any reason why we should object to such a plan, and I should like to see this established on a sure foundation. I have often considered the future welfare of my children, and when I see them before me before me I think seriously on their future condition. I am glad to hear that our Great Father is anxious to assist up by putting us in the way, and promoting our welfare.

A little more, I have not much more to say. We will attend to this subject, and observe how the matter proceeds in the Council; and see whether what is desired will come to pass. This is all I say.

Yet a little more; I wish to say, with regard to our Islands, that in case of our removal, we desire to have them secured to us. I have said enough. (Snake, 1846, p. 21)

It was important to Chief Joseph Snake that the people kept their connection with the islands. That is one strong reason why the people remained on the island, and why the people still own the three islands. He was memorialized by the Georgina Island people by having Chief Joseph Snake Road named after him. It runs the length of the west side of Georgina Island, the longest road there.

Another speech from this time will be presented in the chapter on "Going to School." Again, you will have good reason to respect his words.

The Graveyard on Snake Island: 1865

Snake Island extends southwest to northeast. There is a tiny graveyard on the narrow southwestern peninsula, near the shore on the north side.

We do not know exactly how long Chief Joseph Snake lived, as the year of his birth was not written down on paper. But it is known that he was chief for a very long time. In the *North York Intelligencer* of December 8, 1865, there were recorded the remarks of visitors who viewed a small graveyard on the western part of the island. They saw three or four graves that were protected from the cattle on the island by large stones and logs. Further:

> There was one grave that particularly attracted our attention; it was the last resting place of Caugh Nebagodeen or Joseph Snake, who was for nearly a century Great Chief and Medicine Man of the Chippewas of Snake Island. We had nearly all seen the old Chief years ago, but had not heard of his decease prior to our visit. He had been dead about three years (1862?) and as he left no son to succeed him the chieftainship was left vacant. A grand council of the tribe was then summoned to meet on a certain day, and after the pipe of peace had passed around, and the orators had made their speeches, they proceeded with becoming gravity to elect one of their number to the vacant office. The choice of the tribe fell upon Simpson Big Sail, a noted young warrior and hunter, and from that time to the present he has been recognized as Chief or King of the Indian Isles of Lake Simcoe.

There is some confusion concerning this statement of Chief Joseph Snake not leaving a son to inherit his chiefly title, and of his being chief for "nearly a century." As we have seen, in 1845, there was a Chief Joseph Snake and a Joseph Snake Junior who had five people living in his household. Perhaps somewhere along the line a Chief Joseph Snake had replaced another man of the same name, but outsiders were unaware of this. A similar sort of confusion existed for Chief Yellowhead, and his son William Yellowhead, who eventually replaced him. The mystery continues.

Simpson Big Sail was a grandson of Chief Joseph Snake, and cousin of later Chief Charles Big Canoe. He was chief from 1861 until his death in 1869. His salary as chief increased during that time from $12.50 to $42.53. He would certainly have earned that much and much more.

Not all stories agree that the small graveyard on Snake Island actually holds the last resting place of Chief Joseph Snake. One such story tells of his bones, along with those of six others, including a brother, being located south near Holland Landing, where they lie with no markers showing where they were laid to rest. Perhaps this relates to the harsh winter of 1837–8 in which some Chippewa warriors were forced by the government to stay there as a threat to rebels in the area. In 1965, an archaeological dig was undertaken in the area and a 19th century Aboriginal burial ground with 40 skeletons was unearthed.

The same observers that made the positive comments quoted above were impressed with the quality of the houses of the people, particularly that of the chief (*Newmarket Era*, December 8, 1865):

> The Snake Island settlement seemed to be [in] a flourishing condition and most of the families appeared to be doing very well. The houses were principally built of log and in many cases were large and commodious. We were in several that were favourably well-furnished—one particular, at the Western extremity of the Island—which in point of order and [cleanliness] would compare favourably with the best managed house[s] in the County of York. It was partly built of hewn logs, very neatly put together, with a frame addition, and had four rooms on the ground floor with several above. The walls of the sitting room were paper and the floor scoured till it was spotless white, was neatly covered with beautifully worked mats, while a sofa, chairs, table and a bureau were arranged around the room in good order.

John Snake

As we have seen, John Snake was a good speaker, the orator for his people. He was also a masterful hunter, and a useful person for settlers to know. One such family that was glad of his acquaintance and friendship was the MacLeods. They left their homeland, the Isle of Skye—located off the northwest coast of Scotland—in 1845, and purchased property alongside Yonge Street in what is now the town of Richmond Hill. They were quite fortunate to meet up with John Snake one snowbound winter's day when they were lost despite the use of a compass, trudging south in their snowshoes when they thought that they were walking north. As written by Sherrill MacLaren, based on an early journal written by Martin MacLeod:

> John Snake simply appeared out of the forest. He stared at the Macleod men standing awkwardly on their snowshoes, beaver caps perched on furrowed brows. Then he turned and without a compass pointed out their exact bearings. Martin was astounded and later wrote that John Snake repeated his performance even in poor weather with neither sun nor shadow. He could always lead them immediately to their destination. (MacLaren, 1986, p. 60)

Martin MacLeod "marvelled that John Snake could 'trot through the densest forest with the agility and precision of a fox'" (MacLaren, 1986, p. 60).

The Snakes and the MacLeods became close friends, which benefitted both families:

> As the Snakes' guns were often in disrepair they delighted in borrowing the Macleods' rifles, most careful to return them by evening. The Snakes repaid the kindness by acts, rarely gifts. Once when Martin's dog chased a deer deep into woods and became lost, one of the Ojibwas followed it for two days and eventually brought it home. (MacLaren, 1986, p. 60)

They visited each other's homes. We have a description of what appears to have been John Snake's winter home, which his family shared with his cousin's family. James MacLeod, a good friend of one of John's sons, who taught the settler his Anishinaabemowin language and hunting skills, provided this rare look into a Chippewa wigwam (as recorded by Sherrill MacLaren):

> Their floors were layered with small branches of hemlock, pine, flat leaves and mats. A fire blazed in the centre. Their hunting implements were arranged on hooks attached to poles which supported a covering of birchbark. Outside venison and other meat hung from nearby trees. (MacLaren, 1986, p. 61)

What would prove to be a continuing pattern of friendship between Snake Islanders and their settler neighbours was early established and long lasting.

Chief George McCue

In an 1856 entry in the diary of James Anderson, a Hudson's Bay Company trader who bought pelts from the trappers of Snake Island, this short description appears, referring to his relationship to his friend George McCue during the 1840s:

> George used a dug-out canoe, the only one I have seen in this district. George had long "Uncle Sam whiskers."[14] He camped near our cottage and made me a bow and arrow every year. (Anderson, 1856, "History of the Town of Georgina," ww.lchr.org/a/33/45/History_of_Georgina.html)

George McCue would travel a long way in his pursuit of trade, making his way up the often treacherous waters of the St. Lawrence River to the Hudson's Bay Company's Fort Mingan on the north Quebec shore of the Gulf of St. Lawrence, north of Anticosti Island. McCue was chief from 1872–5, before such time as the community had band councillors to assist the chief.

While he was chief, George McCue had to fight off government attempts to divide up the land on the island into individual plots, and for the people to enfranchise (i.e., lose their Indian status, and their rights under previous treaties and other agreements). With him in this fight at *The Grand General Council of the Chippewas, Munsees, Six Nations etc, etc., Held on the Sarnia*

---

14. "Uncle Sam" was an image on posters encouraging American males to enlist in wars. Among other consistent features of this character was a long white goatee.

Reserve, June 25th to July 3, 1874, was James Ashquabe, later to be a band councillor. He was probably the main orator[15] for his people at that time:

> On Wednesday evening, Ashquabe openly stated that no one at Snake Island wanted to be enfranchised, as they thought "it would be the means to bring them to poverty." As far as the residents of Snake Island were concerned, sufficient progress had been made among their people under the current arrangements, which they were content to retain. Moreover, Snake Islanders considered the reserve to be permanent and did not think that portions of it should be alienated to individual members. (As interpreted by Shields, 2001, pp. 48–9)

Moving to Georgina Island

There was not sufficient good agricultural land on Snake Island for the expansion of farming, so, by the early 1860s, people began to move east to Georgina Island, which was larger. It was land that they owned, so they could move there freely, without worrying about settlers moving in there first.

Traditional Hunting Territories and Land Claims

While the people lived and had their houses on Snake Island or Georgina Island during the nineteenth century, this was not the limit of the territory that they relied upon at that time. They also hunted, trapped, gathered and grew food and medicines on lands that had been used by the people for a long time. These rights had not been officially surrendered or ceded to the federal government. They would have to fight for recognition of their rights there in relation to the Williams Treaties.

As much as the people had long treasured the islands that comprised their land, there was a sense that it was much less than what they had lived on and used earlier. While the government called the islands a reserve, as it was reserved for their use, according to Elder Barbara McDonald, the old chiefs had another name for where they were forced to live: *Shkunamanjinik* ('leftovers').

In 1911, Chief Charles Big Canoe (whose story, mostly from his own words, will be told in the next chapter) along with his fellow chiefs and

---

15. It was a common traditional practice for Indigenous peoples to have a gifted 'orator' to speak for a chief.

members of the Rama and Christian/Beausoleil Island bands, made, not for the first time, legal statements asserting their rights to the land. The following is an excerpt from the claim made by Charles Big Canoe concerning the hunting rights of the people of Georgina Island and Rama:

In the matter of claims for compensation for unsurrendered northern hunting grounds claimed by the Lake Huron and Simcoe Chippewas located at present at Georgina Island, Christian Island and Rama in the province of Ontario and more fully described as the hunting ground lying north of line 45° to the height of land near Lake Nipissing. I, Chief Big Canoe of the Georgina Island Reserve in the county of York, Province of Ontario, Dominion of Canada.

1st do solemnly declare that I am a regular member of the above band of Chippewa Indians, that I was born on Snake Island in Lake Simcoe, County and Province aforesaid, that I am now in my seventy-eighth year and that I have always resided with my people on Snake or Georgina Island Reserves.

2nd With reference to the above claims, I know that my tribe won said hunting grounds from other Indian tribes by reason of our victory over them and that ever since I can remember we were in peaceable and unmolested possession of the said hunting grounds and our fathers before us.

3rd That about the year 1862 I made my first hunting trip in the territory referred to accompanied by my father-in-law the late Chief Joseph Benson Nanigishkung who had a hunting ground limit of his own and upon his death was given to his son, Mr. James Benson Nanigishkung and myself. Said limit was located between the following lakes: Island Lake, Canoe Lake, Little Joe Lake, Potters Lake, Brule Lake and Ke-che-pe-se-ge-kah-me-song, and the Muskoka River which was our North East boundary, Potters and Brule Lakes being our western boundary, bounded by line 45 and to the north to the extreme point on the height of land, which was marked by a very large pine tree which was blazed denoting the boundary line.

4th I hunted regularly in these limits for thirteen years in succession.

5th That we made our camping ground at Canoe Lake, where we dried our furs.

6th The route I took with my father-in-law from the Rama Reserve was by canoe River Severn to Sparrow Lake Portage to Leg Lake portage, Leg Lake to Muskoka Lake to the north of Muskoka River, thence to *Ke-kah-pe-kong* now Bracebridge portage to South branch of Muskoka River to Trading Lake making nine portages between Bracebridge and *non-get-tah-we-gah-mog* (Trading Lake), now called Lake of Bays. Thence portage to Oxtongue Lake portage to Muskoka river, then to Sand Lake, thence Muskoka river to Shallow Lake following Muskoka river to Canoe Lake our regular camping grounds. The trip takes about two weeks from Rama to Canoe Lake.

7th We disposed of our furs to one Alexander Bailey … who was camped at the point where the town of Bracebridge now stands…

12th[16] My people[17] had a clearance at Trading Lake and raised corn and potatoes at this camp and some of my people died, buried at this point on Trading Lake… Many of the Bigwind family died and was buried at Trading Lake, also one of the Snake family. (Big Canoe, Charles, 1911, Department of Indian Affairs, RG10 vol.2838, file 67071-1)

John Bigwind[18] also made a claim in 1911, with especial regard for the island now called Bigwin Island in Lake of Bays (the former Trading Lake). He was concerned, as was Charles Big Canoe, about the protection of the many graves that were on the island, and offshore. Some of those graves are likely those of Snake Islanders.

The Bigsails and Gardening on Snake Island

During the 1880s and 1890s the Indian agent for the band, J. R. Stevenson, made frequent note of the Bigsail family being on Snake Island, and of their having a fairly extensive and well-developed garden.

I have pleasure in mentioning the extensive garden of Mr. Wm. Bigsail, of Snake Island, embracing potatoes, corn, beans, and a great variety of others vegetables, as also a great variety of small fruit, showing good care and cultivation. (Stevenson, 1889, p. 13)

---

16. Numbers 8 to 11 appear to be missing from this text.
17. Here he was speaking of both the Georgina Island and the Rama bands.
18. For a short article discussing the life of John Bigwind, read the South Muskoka Doppler article, "Chief John Bigwind at Bracebridge Falls," February 23, 2022. https://southmuskoka.doppleronline.ca/chief-john-bigwin-at-bracebridge-falls/.

In the *Annual Archaeological Report of 1897–8* it was noted that Paul Big Sail had found and donated to Ontario's provincial museum (now the Royal Ontario Museum) an ancient stone adze (a wood working tool) that was about eight inches long (Boyle, 1898, p. 10).

January 1911 marked the death of a dynamic woman who was born in 1802, and lived most of her long life on Snake Island, where she died at age 108. She was born Sarah or Sally Bird at the Narrows, and was the older sister of Henry Bird Steinhauer (born Shawwahnegezhik; c. 1817–1884), a man who became a well-known translator, educator and preacher for the Methodist Church (Smith, 2013, pp. 245–76). Sally Bird married Thomas Big Sail on June 24, 1832, and she taught her husband how to read through memorizing hymns. They had 10 children, five girls and five boys. She outlived her husband, and six of their children (*Orillia Packet*, February 2, 1911; www.waynecook.com/obits.html).

Sally Big Sail

Snake Island: 1891

In the Indian Affairs accounting for Snake Island in 1891, the community at Snake Island had a significant amount of money held 'in trust'—$24,793.14—coming from the land sale, money they could not access directly. Further, they paid for their expenses (and some of the government's) with the interest on that and other money held 'in trust'—$1,683.63—and still had some left over: $247.18. The population of the community that year was 125.

Chippewas of Snake Island
    In Account with Department of Indian Affairs
        Service
        Capital

By Balance on 30th June, 1890	$24,674.57
Land Sales	$129.73
To Management Fund percentage on collections	$11.16
By Balance on 30th June, 1891, brought down	$24,793.14
Interest	$231.15
Rents	$220.00
Interest on invested capital	$1232.48

To Salaries

Chas. Big canoe, chief	$80.00
Jas. Ashquab, councillor	$21.00
Wm. Ashquab, d[itt]o	$25.00
Jos. Charles, do	$12.00
Geo. McCue, do	$21.00
Noah Snake, do	$9.00[19]

Sundry disbursements

Distribution of interest moneys	$970.05
Services of Wm. Bigsail at election of chiefs.	$2.00
Medical services	$256.50
Relief to destitute Indians	$11.00
Funeral expenses	$3.00
Travelling expenses, Agent Stevenson	$3.00
Paid Wm. Bigsail, for cutting wood for Widow Snake	$5.00
Work on mission house	$9.40
Management Fund, percentage on collection	$2.50
Balance on 30th June, 1891	$247.18
	$1,683.63

By Balance on 30th June, 1891, brought down $247.18

(S.E. Dawson, Sessional Papers, Volume 10, Second Session of the Seventh Parliament of the Dominion of Canada, Session 1892, volume XXV [Ottawa: S. E. Dawson])

A letter dated June 20, 1914, was received by the Indian Affairs Department putting forward a proposal to buy all of Snake Island for a rich

---

19. The reason for the difference in band councillor salaries probably lies in the length of time each served that particular term.

man's summer home, falsely claiming that "There are no Indians living on this island and the island is entirely unsuitable for agricultural purposes" (Indian Affairs RG10, volume 2197, file 39, 739–18). It is probably after some correspondence back and forth that an Indian Affairs official finally declared in a letter dated December 16, 1918, that:

> ... this island belongs to the Chippewa Indians of Georgina Island and Snake Island. It has not been surrendered, and a surrender would have to be obtained from the Indians before any dispositions could be made thereof. (Indian Affairs RG10, volume 2197, file 39, 739-18).

The Snake Name

While the Snake name was frequently found when the people lived on Snake Island, it is less often to be seen or heard on Georgina Island today. This is not because they had smaller families than others, or that a significant number moved away. It is because the Methodist Church found the name offensive, the snake being the one who tempted Eve. So people changed their name to please the church. The new surname that began to appear among Snake descendants was Snache.

Among the descendants of this family is the first Aboriginal Lieutenant-Governor of Ontario (2002–7) and prolific writer on Indigenous issues[20] James Bartleman. In a chapter entitled "Indigenous Roots" in his book, *Seasons of Hope: Memoirs of Ontario's First Aboriginal Lieutenant Governor*, he makes note of 10 generations of his family, his belonging to the eighth. In the fifth generation, Frederick William Benson Nanigishking married Phoebe Ann Snake of Georgina Island His great-grandmother on his father's side was Phoebe Ann Snake of Georgina Island (1878–1918), daughter of Abraham Snake and Martha Goose of Snake Island. Her mother-in-law was born Charlotte Charles from Snake Island (Bartleman, 2016, p. 48). Her father-in-law's first wife was some "unknown Bigcanoe." He also spoke of one of his ancestors as "young John Simcoe," who was born in 1823. His father, also called John Simcoe, fought in the War of 1812. His son John may have been the one named in the 1845 census given above, perhaps

---

20. He has so far written six books, both memoirs and novels: *Out of Muskoka* (2004), *On Six Continents: A Life in Canada's Foreign Service, 1966–2002* (2005), *Raisin Wine: A Boyhood in a Different Muskoka* (2007), *As Long as the Rivers Flow* (2011), *Seasons of Hope: Memoirs of Ontario's First Aboriginal Lieutenant Governor* (2016), and *A Matter of Conscience* (2018).

moving to Snake Island from his father's home in Rama, as some people did. Intermarriage between members of the three related bands was not unusual.

The Cottagers Begin to Move onto Snake Island

In 1919, in an act of compromise and some good business sense, Jacob and Mary Bigsail invited in the first cottager, John Brundle, to build a cabin on the island. By 1935, there were 135 cottages there. In 2021, there were 227 cottage leases on the island.

At some point during the 20th century, the Big Sails left Snake Island, at least one family moving to Sandy Cove (see the "Ash Baskets" chapter), along the southwest shores of Lake Simcoe. Their historical significance to the community is not forgotten.

And when the Chippewas went, so did their major buildings, which were for the most part disassembled on Snake Island and reassembled on Georgina Island. The last building to go travelling in this way was the Big Sail cabin in 1920–1.

The people were good at transporting wood for building across water from one place to another. For summer visitors on the mainland, they would cut and shape the wood for building on the island, and then transport the material to the mainland and construct log-cabin cottages where people could stay on their summer vacations.

In August 1948, Harold McCue, World War II veteran at 34, was given the job of caretaker of Snake Island by the band council. He lived there with his wife and small children. In the chapter "The Crossing," you can read about how in 1949 he had to make heroic efforts just to get food for his wife and children as he had to cross over dangerous ice.

The first hydro lines were extended to the Georgina Island in 1954, telephone lines a few years later. Now the only clear sign that the old settlement was there comes from the small cemetery that contains Chief Joseph Snake's gravesite.

The following is a story about living on Snake Island and enjoying visiting Georgina Island for the annual fall Church Anniversary celebration.

Going to the Church Anniversary
BY HARVEY MCCUE

My family lived on Snake Island. My step-father, Harold, my mother, Bea, and I relocated there from Georgina when I was four years old, in

1948. Harold, or Scobe as everyone on the rez called him, served as the first caretaker of Snake Island on behalf of the band council. We lived in a four-room house that he and Clarence Porte built by hand. Like every other house at Georgina, our small home lacked running water and electricity. Eventually our family grew to include three younger brothers, Mike, Tom and George. When we were still very young, early in the fall, we would all load into our small outboard boat for the trip from Snake Island to Georgina for the annual fall Anniversary celebration. I didn't understand what the church anniversary was for, but I knew that it included a lot of games for both kids and adults, as well as a community feast in the Hall, and a dance.

When the weather was good—sunshine and little wind—the trip between the islands was like a magical ride. Our little boat with a 5 hp Evinrude would ride on top of the smooth, glassy water. We were all by ourselves a mile or so offshore the whole way, no cottagers or fisherman on the lake, just the six of us, watching the sun glinting on the calm water, and pointing quickly to any small or large splashes in the water caused by lake trout that might have surfaced near us as we continued our journey. Of course, if the weather was bad, the crossing was too dangerous and we stayed home, sad that we were missing the good food and good time at the Anniversary.

When we arrived at Georgina, our father knew exactly where to land our little boat. It was on the shore a little north of Archie and Bertha (our Little Gran) Blackbird's small house. When the boat was pulled onto the shore we made our way along a little path that ran nearby Archie and Bertha's house to a small cabin that Scobe inherited from his brother George. We only used the cabin when we were able to make the trip to the Anniversary so it was like a special cottage for us. I can't remember it entirely but I do recall the special cosiness of four of us being tucked into one bed by my mother, something that we all thought was extra-special. The next day we'd all head for the grounds by the Hall to watch and participate in the games and competitions. One memory that stands out is the log-sawing contest that my mother and Elaine McCue competed in. Both women were very young and strong and they quickly showed they knew how to handle a saw as well as anyone.

Of course, the main event for me at least, was the community feast in the basement of the Hall. Tables were covered with freshly caught fried trout and whitefish, baked and fried scone, potato salads, and other foods, enough food for everyone to eat as much as they wanted. The women in the kitchen seemed to work all night making sure the fish never ran out.

For me growing up on Snake Island without neighbours, the community feast was a wondrous occasion—everyone seemed to be there, talking and laughing, and enjoying the tasty food, and reliving the games and competitions earlier in the day. When everyone had eaten, people moved outside into the cooler autumn air, to get a breather before the dance in the Hall. Because we were just children, my mom and dad gathered us up and under a harvest moon with a million stars twinkling in the sky, we walked to our small cabin happy to have made the lake trip to another Anniversary! (*The Georgina Island Storytelling Project*, https://georginaisland.com/writing/going-to-the-church-anniversary-harvey-mccue/)

Edna Porte, Wilene McCue, Loretta Big Canoe, and Delina Vernon cooking for a community Thanksgiving dinner

Repatriation on Snake Island

A sacred event recently took place on Snake Island. This story began when an archaeological dig of assessment was done on a site being developed in Bradford, south of Lake Simcoe, beside the Holland River, during the summer of 2011. Human remains were discovered by an archaeological team that included specially trained Georgina Island archaeologist liaisons Ellie Big Canoe and Lyla Big Canoe. The remains were found to be Algonkian (a language and cultural group to which the Anishinaabe belong), and were dated at about 1500 AD. Four bodies were uncovered, an adult woman, a young adult (at least 18), and two children, one judged as being nine, the other two years old. In 2012, before the chief and council had decided what should be done with the remains, the bones were dug up, smashed and some stolen. It was then decided that the best thing that could be done with what remained was to have the bones repatriated in a safe and sacred place—on Snake Island. This was done with due ceremony in 2014 (Riedner, 2014).

CHAPTER THREE

The People Develop Their Agriculture

One major reason for the people to move to Georgina Island from Snake Island was to engage in agriculture on a larger scale than they had before. The people soon demonstrated that this was an endeavour in which they could be quite successful. Over the years, the agricultural skill and work ethic of the Georgina Islanders meant that many a young man from the island was hired as farmworker on the mainland.

This success growing crops and raising livestock began while the people were still on Snake Island. Not only did the people prepare gardens, but their horses and cows impressed mainland observers in 1865 who visited the island. One such visitor wrote:

> In walking about Snake Island we had good opportunities of seeing the Indian horses and stock, which had the undisputed privilege of going from one side or end [to] the other. We did not learn the number of horses owned by the Chippewas but we saw perhaps a dozen there, most of which were young and in good condition. The cattle, too, of which we saw about forty head, were also in splendid condition and would no doubt be a great attraction, if sold to these Yankee buyers who by the hundreds have scattered themselves over Upper Canada this last summer. (Anonymous, *Newmarket Era*, December 8, 1865)

However, the people were soon going to move to Georgina Island, with greater opportunities for farming being an important factor. At left is a photo of a commemoration gathering of the move,[21] some time in the 1870s.

21. Public domain photograph from "Deanna's Story," Never2old2dream.wordpress, August 26, 2020.

Late Nineteenth Century

By the late nineteenth century, on Georgina Island, agriculture was constantly expanding. As the Indian agent reported in 1885:

> The Chippewas of Georgina and Snake Islands in Lake Simcoe, whose reserve comprises those islands, are giving more attention to stock raising and farming, and every year shews marked progress in both enterprises. The population of the band is one hundred and thirty-four, and they have three hundred and ten acres under tillage, whereof ten acres were newly broken this year. The quantity of produce raised by them amounted to three thousand four hundred and thirty bushels of grain and roots, and they cut also twenty-two tons of hay. (Stevenson, 1885, p. 17)

One year is profiled here to demonstrate the success the people had with livestock and crops, and to show some of the other endeavours the people were involved with that helped them survive and prosper in those days.

Georgina Island, 1917

The *Annual Report of the Department of Indian Affairs for 1917* presented incredibly detailed and intrusive information concerning Indigenous communities in Canada. The people were being monitored to a degree that would have made many of them feel oppressed. The federal government could not have gotten away with such monitoring of Canadian people generally.

That being said, the information is useful in representing the lives of the Georgina community at that time. The following are a few details of Georgina life that were measured and published in the Department of Indian Affairs.

Agriculture

You soon notice, when reading this account, that Georgina was a successful farming community, despite the fact that transporting animals and farm products between the island and the mainland was very difficult. It would become even more so when the water level of Lake Simcoe rose in a few years.

In the meticulous measuring of Indian Affairs we can see the crops that the people grew, especially grains, provided the largest single source of income that year: $1,770.00 of a total $7,732.35 earned. Of a recorded total of 3,497 acres of land on the island, 290 acres were cleared for cultivation. Yields were recorded in bushels, an Imperial measure, with a bushel amounting to roughly 36.4 litres.

Crops Grown

Crop	Acres Cultivated	Barrrels Harvested
Hay (cultivated)	80	Unrecorded
Wheat	40	510
Oats	35	315
Other Grains	9	85
Fodder (not hay)	5	Unrecorded
Hay (wild)	4	Unrecorded
Potatoes	1	30
Peas/Beans	1	5
Total Recorded	**175**	**945**

(Scott, *Annual Report of the Department of Indian Affairs*, 1917, p. 96)

To mill grains, the people had first to cart their harvest down to the shore of the island. Then they had to "ship" it by rowboat across the watery divide, then west to the mouth of the Black River, and then a few kilometres upstream to the mill that still stands today and can be seen in Sutton from the main road. The community had at that time 21 rowboats and sailboats, and three motorboats. Getting the grains to the water involved the 26 carts, wagons and other means of transporting goods that the Georgina people had at that time.

Elder Albert Big Canoe speaks of what many Georgina Island farmers did in the past when they brought the grain to the mill in Sutton:

> Well, there was no company. They were more subsistent farmers. They grew mostly everything for themselves. They'd take that grain and made flour and brought it home. Then they'd buy a bag of salt, a bag of sugar. Big bags, you know, not little ones. For the winter so they could bake and whatever.

People had gardens for their own use, of course, and like many a farm community in Ontario of the time, Aboriginal and non-Aboriginal, they held vegetable garden competitions, and these were seriously contested.

Livestock

The main kind of livestock raised by the Georgina people in 1917 was the kind most easily bred and transported: 294 "Poultry" (the record keepers did not distinguish in their writing between hens and roosters) (Scott, 1917, p. 111). In terms of cattle they had 18 "Milch Cows," 17 "Young Stock," 8 "Steers and Work Oxen" and 20 "Other Stock" (perhaps including oxen?), but no bulls. The value of beef sold (including use for food) was $450.00 (Scott, 1917, p. 130). Horses, like cattle difficult to transport from mainland to island and back, comprised 28 gelding and mares, but no stallions. By 1920, there was one bull and one stallion. They did not need to import horses from the mainland anymore.

Possessions

In terms of some of the main possessions that the people had to report, we have the following figures:

Stone, brick, and frame dwellings	14
Other dwellings	22
Outbuildings	55
Ploughs, harrows, drills, etc.	30
Mowers, reapers, binders, threshers, etc.	69
Carts, wagons, and vehicles	26
Tools and smaller implements (Scott, 1917, p. 104)	78
Motor and sail boats	3
Row boats and canoes	21
Rifles and shotguns	25
Steel traps	130
Nets	11
Tents (Scott, 1917, p. 111)	8

Other Sources of Income in 1917

The third highest source of income (after the $1,437.35 from annuities and interest on trust funds) was the vaguely labelled "Other Industries and Occupations" (Scott, 1917, p. 130). This probably included such potential money earning crafts as making black ash baskets, porcupine quillwork, paddles, axe handles and fish decoys, as the settlers were beginning to get involved with spear fishing, and were also learning about fish decoys from the fishermen and carvers of Georgina Island.

Wages earned amounted to $2,345.00, which probably included what men could make getting involved with logging related activities off of the reserve (Scott, 1917, p. 130).

Although we have seen that the people were recorded as having 25 rifles and shotguns and 130 steel traps, hunting and trapping were not listed as generating any income for the people. Fishing accounted for $100.00 (before the profitable days of fish hut rentals), largely achieved with the 11 nets said to be owned by the people.

Pictures of a Successful Community

Robert W. Dunning, the University of Toronto anthropologist who studied the people in 1958, remarked upon the pictures he saw of Georgina Island people during the period when farming was booming on the island:

> Photographs of the time, which show the present grand-parental generation as youngsters, give a picture of fairly well-equipped farming people with some equipment and well dressed in the costume of the day, the women wearing the "Gibson Girl"[22] type of headdress. In dress and comportment they would appear indistinguishable from any such Ontario rural community. (Dunning, 1974)

By 1931 you could see some changes taking place with farming on the island. There were only 100 acres being cultivated. Wheat had dropped to six acres, producing 72 bushels, but potatoes had grown to five acres, with the production of 175 bushels. Log houses were in the minority. More frame houses had been built.

---

22. The term "Gibson Girl" refers to the pen-and-ink drawings of popular illustrator Charles Dana Gibson in the late 19th century and the early 20th century. She was featured as having big hair piled up high and often wore big hats, as well as beautiful but impractical clothing.

A People of Stories

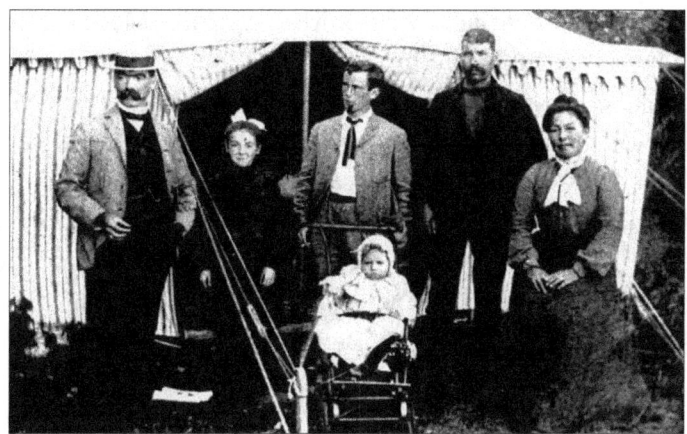

Willie and Emma Ashquabe

Georgina Island Agricultural Fairs

Despite the steady but slow drop in agricultural produce after 1917, the spirit of an agricultural community persisted on Georgina Island. The community had annual agricultural fairs early in September. The following is a newspaper description in the *Newmarket Era* of one such fair, held in 1938:

> Adverse weather conditions failed to deter the large crowd attending the annual agricultural fair on Georgina Island Indian Reserve Wednesday and Thursday of last week. E. J. Sexsmith, agricultural representative of the department of Indian Affairs, officially opened the show.
>
> The sports events were in the charge of the local Indian Agent, O. J. Silver, assisted by the reserve schoolteacher and Lorenzo Big Canoe. Races of every kind were included on the program, but a tug-of-war on horseback, in which the team of Harvey McCue and James York defeated Amos Charles and Stewart McCue in both starts, provided the most amusement for the spectators.
>
> Two groups of Indian residents engaged in a tug-of-war contest in which the team composed of Samuel York, Ben and Lorenzo Big Canoe, James Porte, George McCue, Steve Ashquabe, John Porte and Jim York emerged victorious after a very closely contested struggle.
>
> In the livestock competition Lorenzo Big Canoe and Edward Charles were first with each having ten first prizes to his credit; George McCue, their nearest rival, carried away four first awards.

In the cooking and ladies' work Mrs. Ephraim McCue was in a class by herself by taking 34 first prizes and four second awards. Her nearest competitors were Mrs. A. Big Canoe and Mrs. Arthur Sillaby, each with eleven wins. The baking classes gave Mrs. Alfred Big Canoe four firsts and two seconds. Mrs. Ryerson Snache with three firsts close second was ahead of the third place winner, Mrs. Ephraim McCue.

Transportation facilities included a large motor boat which carried visitors from a dock at Virginia Beach to the Island where a large automobile drove them up to the fairgrounds over a mile away.

A dance was held in the community hall on Wednesday night while on Thursday a concert and dance took place to terminate the activities. (Anonymous, *Newmarket Era*, September 15, 1938, p. 4)

In the summer of 1958, as previously mentioned, anthropologist R. W. Dunning came to engage in research with the people of Georgina Island, disguising the name of the community (as was the practice of researchers of the time) as "Pine Tree" and Snake Island as "Cedar Point." As part of his research, he engaged in comparing some of the fields that had been referred to in the report of 1917. He reported that the large fields of wheat, oats, other grains, peas, beans and potatoes were no more. The farming world had changed, the small-scale farmer did not have the opportunities of earlier days, and the people had adapted to that change.

Helping the "Poor Indians"

Now, despite the great success that the people of Georgina Island had as farmers, and as being quite capable of providing their own food by various means, there were always mainlanders who thought that the "poor Indians" must be starving out there on the island. Elder Albert Big Canoe tells one such story of a deluded mainland woman:

There used to be an old farm lady—I don't know how old she was— she knew my dad and she'd come down to the boat and she'd bring drippings. Cans of ... I don't know what kind ... like grease. Give it to the poor Indians sort of thing. Because back then, a lot of them used to use those drippings on bread, toast. Pork or beef. That was in the fifties. He used to just laugh at her. But he'd take it. He wouldn't insult her. We never used it.

Grazing Mainland Cattle

One way in which the people made money in agriculture at this time was to rent out their fields to graze herds of cattle from the mainland. This would happen in the spring. As many as 200 cows would be brought over in one day. There was no large ferry then, so other means had to be sought out. The cattle would be transported in a barge that could hold perhaps from six to 10 cows at a time. The cows would be shooed off of the barge in the shallow waters beside the island, where they would swim and wade their way to shore, with a little help from the Georgina Island herders. Once on the island, the cattle would be rounded up by the families involved and herded inland, where they would eat to their hearts' content in the fields and underbrush of Georgina Island. It wasn't easy work for the people of Georgina Island to be involved with, but no major cattle catastrophes were ever recorded.

Photo credit: "From Mission to Partnership Collection: Big Canoe," circa 1900, 93.049P1858N, United Church Archives Digital Collection.

CHAPTER FOUR

Charles Big Canoe Tells a Story

Chief Charles Big Canoe

Chief Charles Big Canoe (*Keche* [big] *Chemon* [canoe]) figured that he was born on Snake Island in April 1834 (see below). He died in May 1930 at age 96, although it was reported at the time of his death that he was 99. He was the grandson of Joseph Snake, and in 1881 became the fifth elected chief (following Simpson Big Sail, George Charles, George McCue, and Thomas Big Canoe), being elected for that position seven times until 1911. That amounted to 30 years of service to his people. For 40 some years he was the local Methodist preacher as well. He also was the first president of the Grand Council of Indian Chiefs of Ontario. In addition to that he was also a respected life member of the York Pioneers and Historical Society, known in that organization for his lively and informative presentations about the history of his people.

Although it would be easy for members of settler society to think of him as a good example of an "assimilated Indian," one who accepted the ways of living and thinking of mainstream Canadian society, that would be far from the truth. He was a defender of his people's rights. A classic example of this occurred when a *Toronto Star Weekly* reporter who was known by the by-line of "La Cerise (the Cherry)," in an article with the condescending, convoluted, and lengthy title of "Ojibway Indians of Georgina Island in Lake Simcoe; A Happy and Contented Colony of 130 Members—Old Chief Big Canoe One of Nature's Gentlemen, Who lives in a Well-Furnished Modern Home and Idolizes His Grandchildren, Just Like any White Grandfather would do," made the following questioning statement: "The Government gave you this island to the Indians, didn't they?"

Chief Charles Big Canoe's apt reply was "Oh, no! We reserved this island when we sold our other property" (La Cerise, 1915, p. 7). His grandfather Joseph would have been very proud of him that day.

Despite his being a Methodist preacher, Chief Charles Big Canoe both respected and loved the traditional stories of his people, as can be seen in the preface he contributed to *Algonquin Indian Tales*, a book that was written by his friend Egerton Ryerson Young (father of the man who collected and saved the important story about Chief Big Canoe that the latter would tell much of his life):

> Dear Friend: Your book of stories gathered from among my tribe has very much pleased me. My reading of them brings us the days of long time ago when I was a boy and heard our old people tell these tales in the wigwams and at the campfire." (Young, 1903, p. 3)

Chief Charles Big Canoe's Story[23]
INTRODUCTION
WRITTEN BY E. RYERSON YOUNG, JR.

One of the most distinguished guests at a big camp-meeting held on Christian Island, Georgian Bay, was an old Indian chief, "Keche Chemon," Charles BigCanoe, of Georgina Island, Lake Simcoe. He has been a successful chief and a notable Christian for many years and was highly honored by both the State and his Church. He was one of the most acceptable preachers at the Camp-meeting and was eagerly listened to by both whites and Indians. But the young people were particularly interested in his love story, which also involved his conversion; and, getting up a supper for him one night, they asked him to tell them of his early life.

"Now you nice young ladies," said Chief BigCanoe, in his gracious and chivalrous manner, "who got up this fine supper, you listen and I'll tell you of my early days and how I learned to write letters and how that helped me to win a very fine young lady for my wife."

Then in the liveliest and most dramatic fashion, the old Chief told the following story of his life and courtship.

CHARLES BIG CANOE'S STORY
BY CHARLES BIG CANOE

I must begin at the beginning. I was born in the year 1834, in the month of April. How do I come to know my age when we had no family records? Well, an old white gentleman, a good Christian man, came to live with the Indians about the year 1827 and he taught school at Orillia. That is what

---

23. This is copied from an unpublished manuscript.

the town is called now but the Indian name is: '*Mechekahning*,' which means, "The Narrows," and by that name was known for a long time. Three bands of the Chippewa nation lived in the district between Orillia and Coldwater, Lake Couchiching and Georgian Bay. Their school house and church were in Orillia, their principal town. Here the children were taught during the week and services were held in the church every Sunday. By and by the Government asked the Indian to surrender Orillia and Coldwater, which they finally did.

CHARLES BIGCANOE

Then the three bands separated. Chief Yellowhead went to Rama Reserve, where the village now stands. Chief John Assance went to Beausoleil Island, Georgian Bay, and there settled his followers, and Chief Joseph Snake, with his band, settled at Snake Island, Lake Simcoe. So the three bands separated, the school was broken up and William Law, the old schoolteacher, went to Newmarket, where he worked at his trade of shoemaker, in that village.

By and by the Snake Island band got stronger in population and they advertised for a teacher. Old William Law answers and came to Snake Island as a teacher for the Indians. He was well received, for Chief Joseph Snake and other Indians knew him when he was teaching in Orillia.

This William Law told my mother that I was about three years old at the time of the McKenzie rebellion, which was in the year 1837. My mother said that I was born about the time the frogs came out of their winter quarters. So it must have been in April, 1834, that I was born.

By and by Jacob Charles was appointed Local Preacher at Snake Island, and William Snake was made Local Preacher at Rama and so were Joseph

Benson and Joseph Shilling of the same village. They had all gone to school at *Mechekahning*, and that showed that William Law had some fruits when he taught there.

But my grandfather did not believe in school and I was glad when he kept me out, for I would rather be shooting birds and squirrels with my bow and arrows than be confined in a school house all day.

I remember when my father was sick. It was winter time and the doctor who came to attend him was Dr. Barton. I remember watching his horse coming across the ice, galloping all the way. It was a fine saddle horse. That was the way they travelled in those days. The preacher and the doctor all went on horseback.

My father died and I remember my mother gathering us children (three boys, Thomas Big Canoe, Paul and myself, Charles; and two sisters, Ann and Sarah) and telling us we were poor. But we had a cow, a whitehead with no horns, and she had a bull calf. Thus we had milk for our family. We had pigs that summer and we planted corn to fatten the pigs in the fall. We also planted potatoes. Many a day my mother would send me to hoe the weeds out of our corn and potatoes. Old Calvin Ames, a kind farmer, used to come over and show us boys how to clean our potato and corn patch. Two of us boys stayed with my mother and also the girls; but Thomas, the eldest, went to live with our grandfather. When there was nothing for me to do I would go to my grandfather's house and stay there and sometimes I would stay there all night, but my mother did not like that. She wanted me to come home at night. When I was able to steer the canoe with a paddle, my grandfather took me when he went spearing fish, shooting ducks and hunting deer in the Holland River for many deer and ducks fed there in the marshy ground.

The school was in operation and William Law was there; but my grandfather did not give me a chance to go. The other children of the village at Snake Island attended regularly but I did not.

But one day, which was rough, windy, stormy, when I was thirteen or fourteen years old, I went to school. I saw something done in school that attracted my attention and made me see that there was something in school that I would like to learn. The teacher did not seem to notice me because I did not go regularly to school. I saw my cousin, Simpson Big Sail, take a piece of shingle, about three by four inches, shave it clean with his knife and then write on it. I was sitting behind him and he did not know that I was watching him. After awhile he had filled the shingle with writing. There was a little boy going about and the teacher did not seem to notice the little fellow as he was playing in the room. Simpson caught this little toddler and whispered something into his ear. I did not hear what he was saying to the little boy, but he gave the piece of shingle to him, and the boy went straight to one of the girls across the room. I watched and watched that girl. She was very careful not to let the teacher see that shingle. She would bow her head and look at that shingle. That was enough for me; for this was evidence to convince me that there was something in school. I stayed until the school was out and made up my mind that I must start to go to school. I told my grandfather and he got very cross with me when I said I was going to school. My mother and grandmother did not say anything to me. So the next day I put on my best clothes and went to school. I told the teacher that I was going to attend.

"All right," he said, "I will do the best I can for you."

He called me to come in front of him together with the little boys and the little girls. They all said "A B C," and the teacher wanted me to say the same after them. The school made fun of me, especially the girls. My courage failed me. I could not stand this fun-making and so I did not go to school the next day.

I said to myself, "What shall I do now?" I was between young man and boy. I was badly disappointed.

I went to my cousin Simpson after school and asked him if he could come to my house every night and teach me how to write. He said that he would. I told him that I would pay him for his trouble. He was very pleased to come, and came that evening a candle light. There were no coal oil lamps in those days, only tallow candles.

I told Simpson that I did not care to learn A B C; "all I want you to teach me is how to write and nothing else." He laughed at me. "You've got to learn A B C and the rest of your letters before you can learn to write. You must commence where I did," he said.

The reason that I was so anxious to learn to write was because I wanted to talk to the girls through writing. I though in my foolishness that I could learn to write without mastering my letters and also that I could learn to write in a few days. Simpson started me every night with the A B C, and so on, and I worked hard to learn what I was taught and it was not long before I could read a little. I kept on studying the lessons that he left me so that I would be able to say them when he came again. I worked every night and every chance

I had during the day and soon could read fairly well.

"That is very good," he said, one night, when I read my lesson to him, but while I read the lesson to please him, I did not understand what I was reading. I asked him what it all meant. He explained some words to me but at last he said, "You will have to go to the schoolteacher and ask him to tell you the meaning of that word."

Now, at this time, I was not ashamed to go to the teacher and ask him the meaning of that word. From time to time, I would go to the teacher's house and ask him the meaning of this word and that word.

"You had better come to school now," said the teacher, "I can handle you better there."

I did go for a few hours every day, for I was busy hoeing corn and potatoes, I was always busy doing something to help my mother.

Shortly after this my mother married again, to John Elliott, who was a widower. He was very good to us boys and girls and used us the same as if we had been his own children. He relieved us greatly from working for my mother at home. So I was able to work out amongst the farmers.

When I was seventeen years of age I was asked to work for a Surveyor. I was glad to join his party for I wanted some money to buy some clothes because I wanted to look good as well as to write to the girls.

It was in the month of May that I was hired and it was for the summer. The surveyors were called "Dennis and Bolton" and their office was in the city of Toronto. The Indians of Saugeen and Owen Sound had surrendered their peninsula between Georgian Bay and Lake Huron. Six survey parties were sent out, each to lay out a township. We stayed until the 15th of November. I was paid one dollar and twenty-five cents a day. I was with that survey party for four years in succession. We did not spend our money; we were in the bush all the time. We only bought a little clothing that we needed and this was supplied by our boss, Mr Gossage. So we could come home every fall with all our money, but we had to go to Toronto to draw it. I am sorry to say that money did not do me any good. I spent all that money in foolishness as except what I gave my mother, my brother Paul and my sisters, Ann and Sarah. I was spending myself in a bad life and going with bad company. Whiskey was plentiful and cheap. I gave my mother a good deal of trouble, for she did not like me to go with bad company or to drink firewater.

One day, my mother said to me. "You must make up your mind to live alone, by yourself." I did not understand what she wanted me to do. "To live alone?" I said, "I do not understand you."

"I must tell you plainly," she said. "You must get married. You must break away from you evil companions and build a house and live with your wife." "I am not able to keep a wife," I told her. "I have no money to build a house."

I thought over what my mother had advised. I knew that she must be right, for I had often heard her praying for me and for the rest of her children. I knew that religion and the Christian life were good and that I ought to be a Christian and join the church. I belonged to the choir and sang in the church every Sunday and heard the preaching Sunday after Sunday, but I had not become a Christian. I was very serious and much troubled by my mother's advice.

I thought of the trouble I had given myself to learn how to write and to read. I did not get much rest until I could read and write: and as I mastered reading and writing, I thought that I might master this marrying business too.

At this time my grandfather, Chief Joseph Snake received notice that a new church was to be dedicated at Rama and the church opening was to be on September 18th. The year was 1857. My grandfather was getting old with the infirmities of old age. He came to me and, giving me two dollars, told me to go to the Church Opening for him and to represent him at the opening of the new church.

I felt very small at that time, especially to go in my Grandfather's place and represent him. My two brothers were older than I. I am the youngest of three brothers. Why did he not send Thomas, the eldest of the three brothers, to represent him on this great day of the opening of a new church? But both of my brothers, Tom and Paul, were indulging heavily, drinking whiskey, and he could not trust them to represent him. So, finally, I accepted the two dollars and the commission to represent him at the Church Opening at Rama.

I reached Rama the day before the opening of the new church and went to the Chief, Joseph Benson, and delivered to him the two dollars that my grandfather had sent. I gave him to understand that I would not speak in public and that I wished to hand over the money to the Treasurer and to explain where it came from. The Chief kindly relieved me of this trouble and, after the dedication services, I came back to Snake Island. I took the boat, "Lady of the Lake," at Orillia and came to Belle Ewart. Some of the Rama people came along on the same boat. They came to visit our people at Snake Island. Among them was Chief Joseph Benson, his wife and his daughter, Elizabeth Benson.

But, oh, she was a sweet young lady! I did not feel that I was worthy to speak to her. She was from such a very respectable family and her father, the Chief, a Local Preacher and the Interpreter for the Missionary. We were introduced to each other but I did not say much to her. I was afraid to, for I knew she was a good young lady and a Christian. I saw something of her when she was at the Island but I did not talk with her. Then they all went back to Rama.

Then I thought to myself, "This is the time to make use of your writing, to talk to this young woman, Elizabeth Benson. If you feel unworthy to talk to her personally because she belongs to such a good respectable, religious family, you can write to her." But I kept putting it off. Finally, in the month of September, one year after I met her on the "Lady of the Lake," I made the attempt to write to her, saying that I could talk to her through letters, and say to her what I could not say in person. I started this letter but it took me a long time to finish it. It was hard work to get my words right. At last the letter is written. I mailed the letter. The letter is gone by the post. I was very anxious about my letter after I had mailed it, for fear that I did not word it right. I do not know how often I went to the Post Office, looking for a reply. But at last it came:

"I received your welcome letter," she said, "I am unable to answer your letter by letter. I understand it all what is means. So you will come and see me before my father and my mother, to talk over the matter contained in your letter. Do not make delay. Come at once."

I was afraid to go now because of the way she had worded her letter. I was afraid to talk to her before her father and mother. I would rather see her alone.

But I was on the next boat that went to Orillia and went on to Rama to see her. It was still day-light when I arrived: so I waited in the woods until it was dark. Then I walked up to the house and knocked at the door. The door opened and there she stood, Elizabeth!

"I thought you would come to-day," she said.

Her parents, who were with her inside, smiled. I felt good and strong, for her parents looked so pleased with everything. And all the time I was with them, they used me right.

The next day, when I was with Elizabeth in the house, she brought my letter to me.

"We must now come to a point," she said. "Here is your letter. I understand from your letter that your purpose is to seek me for a life partner, that I should live with you and you with me, as long as this life will last. This is the reason why you have come to see me?"

"Yes," I said

"I am willing to live with you, rich or poor," she said: "providing you will answer to my satisfaction three questions that I will put before you."

"Oh, what is it she wants?" I said to myself. I thought that she was so sweet and I loved her so that I would promise her anything, if, she would only promise to come and live with me.

"The first question is this," she said to me: "'Are you ready to give up using intoxicating drink and be a sober man?' You must do so if I am to live with you. The second question is, "'Are you willing to give up your evil companions?' You must choose between them and me; for you cannot have both. And then as people cannot go together happily unless they be agreed in their heart thoughts, my last question is, 'Are you willing to become a Christian and join the Church for all your life?' I am a Christian and love Jesus and the best way to keep his religion is to join the Church and attend it regularly. So I want to know if you are willing to be a Christian and live your religion?"

I hung my head down for some time and I did not know how to answer her. "You have given me very hard questions," I said, at last, to her, "I cannot answer them off-hand."

"They are not hard questions," she replied. "They are good and you know it: and they are right. They can only do you good, if you keep them."

"I must have time to think them over before I answer you," said I, "I must ask you to give me time to answer these hard questions."

"How much time do you want," she asked: "one month, two months, three months?"

"No, no," said I, excitedly and swinging my arms around the sky: "Not that long, just one day, from this sun-set to the next sun-set, then I will answer your questions."

"All right, take your time," said she: "I'll await your answer."

I did not get much sleep that night. Those questions bothered me. However was I to answer them? I did not eat much breakfast; for those questions were ever before me and so was she. They were so hard and she was so sweet. The questions were good, as she said; but if I answered her as she wished, however was I to keep them?

After breakfast I left the house and went into the woods. I walked a long way into the bush and intended to stay there all day. Every time I thought of those questions, I was troubled. How was I to keep from drinking whisky? All the men around me, Indians and whites, especially those that worked in the bush and in the fields, drank it. How could I keep away from my evil companions, or my own brothers? I knew the Christian religion was good, for I was raised by a Christian mother.

When I got away in the bush another spirit came into me and I said: "I did not come to this place to have any person advise me what to do." I walked on faster than ever and my thoughts said, "Better go right on, walk fast, get right away and never see that young woman and her hard questions again. Who is she anyway? What kind of life would a man live with a woman who would dictate to him like that?" But I stopped. My heart cried out against that thought. She was so lovely, so straight-forward and honest; she was so good and so true, and she was so sweet. There was just no one on earth like her. And after all, if we are to live happily together, her questions were right and she only asked me to walk the good way. But I only walked on farther into the bush and was more troubled than ever.

At last I sat down on a fallen log and thought of my trouble. And, oh, how I was troubled! The sun rose and shone straight down on me through the trees and I knew it was noon; but I thought that I was not far enough in the woods and wanted to be sure I was alone. So I got up and walked still farther into the woods. In these deep woods I seemed to hear my mother's voice and I seemed to see her on her knees in prayer for me. I could hear her praying again the words I had often heard from her lips. She was praying to our Heavenly Father about me, and pleading His promise to help in time of need and to lead in the right way. So I said to myself, "My Heavenly Father can help me answer these hard questions." I knelt down by an old log and prayed. But I got no peace. There was still the thought to get up and go away and never to come back. I did go on deeper into the bush. Then I stopped and prayed again and still no answer. The trouble was still in me and I was sore with it. I had a big silver watch and when I looked at it, it was three o'clock. Then I thought and prayed some more but I said that it must be settled then and there, for the time to give my answer was not far off. I prayed again to my Heavenly Father to help me. Then I heard my mother's words: "Trust in the Lord and do good and he will help." I said, "If the Lord will help me, I can answer all those hard questions and keep them, too! When I said that

I felt that the Lord had answered my prayer. I felt it in my heart: I felt so relieved and light and happy. And I felt that the good Lord was near me. I thought that the trees were smiling at me. It seemed to me that the Lord said clearly in my mind, "Fear not, I will be with you."

I hastened back to Elizabeth, rejoicing. I was not afraid to answer her hard questions now, for I know that my prayer has been answered and that God would help me to answer them.

She was pleased to see me return.

"I will answer all your questions now," I said to her: "to abstain from the use of intoxicating drink; to break away from my evil friends, and to be a Christian; for I believe my Heavenly Father has accepted me to be His child."

Then I told her of my prayer and the answer in the bush. She went and told her father and her mother; and they told their preacher, the Rev. George McDougall, who was then in charge of the Rama Indian Mission.

I did not expect to be married right away. I wanted Elizabeth to visit my people and then we would arrange a wedding, with all our people present; but Mr. McDougall did not see it that way. "You must marry that girl before you take her away from this village," he said to me.

I was very agreeable to this and told him to see her parents. So the next evening, the 26th day of September, I was married to Elizabeth Benson in Chief Benson's House.

"The next day I took my wife to Snake Island, to my mother's house, where we lived for four months. Then we lived with my brother Paul for two or three months.

"Can we not make a home of our own on your lot?" Elizabeth said to me one day.

"My grandfather has given me five dollars to buy anything I want," I told her. I went to Mr. George Johnson on the mainland, the next day, and bought one thousand feet of pine lumber. I picked very wide boards. I hired a team to bring the lumber to the shore. My lot was on Georgina Island and I got the lumber up myself.

I got up on the bank and looked at my lot, No. 6, Concession 1. It was a beautiful hard wood bush, mostly maple and heavy timber. I laid my axe against an ironwood tree and I prayed to my Heavenly Father to establish my house there and to give me strength to work the place. I fully believed at that hour that my Heavenly Father answered my prayer. I felt in my heart and soul that God was going to help me and my faith was getting stronger all the time. While underbrushing, I was singing all the day. After I have made a little opening, I built my camp for logs high and put a roof on, using the timber that I had brought over from the mainland.

One fine morning I told my wife I was going to see my lot and brought her over from Snake Island to Georgina Island. She was very glad to see the log cabin I had made and we made our first home there. We tapped many maple trees and started at once to make sugar. We made a lot that year. After the lake opened we had lots of fish, wild ducks and pigeons.[24] The pigeons came in clouds in those days. We had plenty of everything in the way of food for our own use. So our house was established and we were very happy."

BACK TO THE AUDIENCE AND THE STORYTELLER

The young people applauded the Chief and crowded around him, asking him many questions. "Haven't I told you enough for one time?" he asked, laughingly. "But you haven't your wife with you," said one of the young women.

"No," said the Chief, his eyes still shining, for his heart was full of faith and love, "she is not with us now but with Jesus, whom she loved and served faithfully all her days. She was a good woman and lived only for that. She helped me in all my religious life. The land was better on Georgina Island and the Indian families followed me and by 1862 they were all on the new island. That year I was appointed Class-leader and Local Preacher. In all my work for the good of my people, my wife helped. She was a leader in every good thing among the women. We soon had a new and large and better house and our home was always the home of the visiting missionary. A Church was built on the island in 1864 and a very successful camp-meeting was held on the island that same year. In 1881 I was elected Chief of my band and my wife's good life and good judgment were always a source of help and strength to me. On the 26th of April, 1893, my wife said goodbye to us and, full of faith, she went home to be with Jesus. Her body is buried in the little graveyard by the Church she so loved. Oh, she was a sweet young lady."

"She was a saint," declared one of the enthusiastic girls.

"Yes," acknowledged the Chief, "she was a good woman."

---

24. These would be the now-extinct passenger pigeons.

E. Ryerson Young's Final Note

New Year's, 1928, as we write, Charles Big Canoe, though ninety-three years of age, is with us, full of life and interested in all that goes around him. His sight only seems to have failed him and the Chieftainship of his band has passed to another, but, to the old man's great joy, it was passed to his son, John, who, with his brother Albert and their families, see that their good father receives the best of care. E. Ryerson Young (Jr.)

Buried on the Island

Chief Charles Big Canoe died on the mainland, so he had to be taken by a rowboat to be buried on Georgina Island. His funeral was delayed by a day as the waters—deeper than when he was a boy—were too dangerous to risk on his last journey to the island. No hearse could make it to the island, so he was taken to his grave in a horse-drawn wagon. His long obituary printed on May 9, 1930, page 7, of the *Newmarket Era* ended with the words that he was "the best known and respected Indian in this century."

CHAPTER FIVE

Going to School

The people long have had contact with the formal schooling of mainstream society, but they still benefit from instruction in traditional ways, as they always have. Their first significant contact with this new kind of education began in the 1820s. By 1829, a Methodist mission school had been built on Snake Island, and when the people returned to the island from the Narrows in the 1840s, they would be taught there.

Chief Joseph Snake Speaks about Education
The year was 1846. The Upper Canada government wanted to send the children of several Anishinaabe communities to an early form of residential school. It was the soon-to-be-established Manual Labour School at Alnwick, on the land of the Alderville First Nation, by the shores of Rice Lake. In late July of that year, the leaders of several First Nations of southern Ontario met with the government officials in response to this and other controlling proposals they were trying to impose on the people. Chief Joseph Snake spoke of his rightful concerns regarding having the children of the community taught so far away from home. He wanted them to remain nearby:

> My Chiefs
> We have for a long time heard of these High Schools, and the more we hear of the plan, the better we like it. We had a Council about it. The one of the Superintendents who passed, mentioned the subject; we were very much pleased with the plan; so we held a Council and agreed to give Two Hundred Dollars a year (£50).
> I will tell you the sentiments of the Chiefs of my people. They are rather disposed to wish that the High School should be on Lake Simcoe. In the event of any disturbance among the Whites,[25] the High

---
25. Chief Joseph Snake was probably referring to the then relatively recent Rebellion of 1837–8.

School at a distance might be destroyed; whereas if it is back in the central part of the Country, it would be safer.

This is the opinion of the Scugog [sic—Simcoe][26] chiefs. And this is the reason why I said that I did not know when my children would be sent. This is all I have to say. (1847, p. 27)

The Manual Labour school was constructed in 1848, with a charge of $64 per student placed on each community. The school was largely funded through the annuity payments of the bands involved, as well as through butter and cheese made and sold by the students at the school. In its initial form, the school only lasted for six or seven years, with students from several communities, including Snake Island, attending.

Schooling on Georgina Island and Snake Island in the Nineteenth Century
THE TEACHERS
During the nineteenth century all of the school teachers for the community were men.

The first face of formal schooling for the children of the people was that of William Law, as you have read in the words of Charles Big Canoe in the previous chapter. He taught them when they were at the Narrows in the 1830s, and kept on teaching them when they returned to Snake Island. He was their teacher until 1868. Like those who would follow, he was paid both by the band (from the interest of the money that was held "in trust" for them by the federal government) and by the Wesleyan Missionary Society, the two major funders of Snake Island and Georgina Island education during the nineteenth century.

He was replaced by Charles Grills (or Grylls), who taught the children of the community from 1868 to 1880, with a break of a few years.

Then the children had an Anishinaabe teacher. For at least three years (1877, 1878 and 1879), Alfred McCue stood in front of the classroom and gave lessons. He may have been temporarily replacing Grylls for those three years. Alfred McCue was from the Curve Lake band, and would later teach in his home reserve in the 1880s and for the Anishinaabe of Beausoleil Island in the 1890s.

The next teacher involved with the school for a long time was Robert Moyes, who was there from 1881–8 (when he resigned), and again from

---

26. This is a mistake made by those involved who published this, not by the chief.

1892 until 1897, when he was "removed." There is no readily available official record of why it was thought best for the students that he no longer teach them.

THE SCHOOL INSPECTION:
GEORGINA ISLAND STUDENTS ACHIEVE A HIGH MARK

In May 1884, David Fotheringham, the school inspector for North York (the name then given to the territory north of Toronto to Lake Simcoe), made a visit to the school, and his positive report concerning the performance of the Georgina Island children was published in 1886 in the *Sessional Papers of the Legislature of the Province of Ontario*, volume 2:

> School House—Log, twenty-one feet wide, twenty-five feet long and eight feet high; very cold in winter. A new one, frame, to be erected this season by the Indian Department...
>
> Appliances—Very limited. One small and poor blackboard, a map of the world only,[27] with some old tablets ... some pews from church the only desks, with a few benches for seats, neither comfortable nor suitable...
>
> Subjects Taught. Reading, writing, arithmetic, and a little grammar and geography, all in English, though the teacher, Robert Moyes, can speak in their own language, Ojibbeway.
>
> Order and spirit—All I could desire
>
> Work—Reading, creditable, fairly intelligent and with good accent and pronunciation. Writing, superior, both as to being uniform and free. Few schools in North York equal in writing... Singing, better than in most public schools, not only in sweetness of voice, but in expression and training.
>
> Number of pupils present, ten boys and eleven girls. On the island about thirty children and one hundred adults. (Fotheringham, 1886, pp. 126–7)

Over the years, people from the mainland would often comment positively about the singing of the children and adults of Georgina Island.

---

27. He recommended that they get a map of Canada as well.

Investing in Education

During Moyes' time the people of the community made two significant investments in the education of their children. In 1884, the Indian agent wrote:

> That they are not indifferent to the importance of educational facilities being furnished their children is shown by the band have had a very commodious building erected, during the year, at their own expense, for school purposes, at a cost of about $600, and the pupils in attendance are reported to be making excellent progress in their studies. (1884, p. 16)

The next year the community would pay for a second storey to be added to the Methodist Mission house, where the teachers lived.

Chief Charles Big Canoe

We have seen that learning to read and write helped Chief Charles Big Canoe win as his bride the chief's daughter from Rama. Although he had little formal education himself, as a chief he was dedicated to the children getting the best education possible. During his time as chief, two teachers were "removed" from the school by the Methodist authorities: Robert Moyes in 1897 and J. H. Prousser in 1909. We know that Chief Big Canoe played an active role in the dismissal of Prousser, although the head of the Methodist Mission initially disregarded his complaints as the person complaining was "Indian" (Miller, 1996, p. 189). Chief Big Canoe's critical remarks included the statement that Prousser's own children set a bad example for the Georgina Island students by stealing and swearing, and that Prousser would not "obey the Rulings of the council of this Reservation" (Big Canoe to A. Sutherland, August 7, 1907, as quoted in Miller, 1996, p. 475, fn 14).

One sign of the success of schooling on Georgina Island is that in 1916, out of a band population of 109, 100 could speak English, and 80 could write in the language (1917, p. 194). As a reference for future band members interested in the language, it would have been very useful if Indian Affairs had also given the numbers of the speakers and writers of their native language Anishinaabemowin as well, but that was not important to the federal officials at that time. We can, however safely say that the language still flourished and there were many fluent speakers. Everyone would know something about the language, even though the language of the school was English.

Residential Schools

Despite having their own day school on Georgina Island, some of the Georgina Island children were forced to experience residential schools as well, notably Shingwauk Industrial School near Sault Ste. Marie (run by the Anglican Church, and operating from 1873 to 1970), and, nearer to home, but still far away, the Mount Elgin Industrial School in Muncey in southwestern Ontario. The Mount Elgin school had been built in 1851, and was active until 1946. It was initially run by the Wesleyan Methodists, the same people responsible for the day school on Georgina Island. In the *Annual Report of the Department of Indian Affairs for 1915*, there are the following figures:

> Georgina Island
> Number of pupils enrolled at day school: 25
> Average attendance at day school: 16
> Number attending Shingwauk Home: 3
> Number attending Mount Elgin Industrial: 2
> (1917, p. 542)

That year there was a truant officer, who was paid $6 to see that students were attending school (1916, p. 895). The next year there were two Georgina Island students at Shingwauk and six at Mount Elgin (1917, p. 530). Unfortunately, the published annual reports do not give figures for other years.

The teacher that served as a replacement on Georgina Island for a four-month period in 1915 was a Mrs. A. J. Taylor. Given that is a Georgina Island surname, she may have been a band member, the first on record teaching her own people.

Cynthia Wesley-Esquimaux, a Georgina Island band member and a person very successful in the educational world as a university professor and respected scholar, tells of growing up with her mother's stories of her experience at Shingwauk (which her mother endured for eight years). One such story was particularly striking:

> I remember when I was a young girl being forced to kneel every morning with all the other girls, the matron was a large black woman, and I'll never forget how every morning, she would make us kneel and pray, and she would say very loudly, "God bless these

little savages," and we always wondered why she said that, who was she to call us savages. (Wesley-Esquimaux, 2010, p. 59)

Lorenzo Big Canoe: Boilermaker, Teacher, and Chief
Although he would eventually become the chief (from 1947 to 1956, and then again from 1959 to 1963), Lorenzo Big Canoe first showed his abilities to lead as a teacher. He was one of the first generation of Aboriginal teachers who acquired the piece of paper necessary to teach in provincially/federally mandated schools. After graduating from Albert College, a prestigious private school (from pre-kindergarten to high-school graduation) in Belleville, he received a special permit to teach. Going to university could have made him lose his Indian status and therefore his right to live on Georgina Island. He began his teaching career in the nearby Anishinaabe community of Beausoleil/Christian Island, teaching there from 1923 to 1926. From there he taught at the Protestant school in the Mohawk community of Caughnawaga (Kahnawake), Quebec, where he worked from 1926 to 1930. He met his Mohawk wife there. Two of his sons were born there.

Education was not his only career. He also worked successfully for a while for the T. Eaton Company as a sports salesman and buyer. Later on, he on became a boilermaker, a skilled trade that he encouraged and helped other Georgina Island young men get involved with, another way in which he was a leader of his community.

He came back to his community to take over his uncle's farm in 1938. His cousin did not want to do it. Although he came back to farm, he ended up in the 1940s engaged in teaching in his own community. According to his son, Albert Big Canoe, he was asked to do so as a teacher that had been there had left. Albert and his brother Andrew were both students of his, but they were not given special treatment as teacher's sons:

My dad, unfortunately he didn't come home to teach. He was home a little while. The teacher left. So they recruited him to teach. My brother hated it because in those days there was corporal punishment. And he had to do that. He'd use a switch. And he'd make the offender go out and cut it.

The Switch
Lorenzo Big Canoe was not unique in the community in using the switch,

and in making the offender go out and cut the switch. As Sam York tells the story about his grandmother, perhaps the trip out to cut the switch was a test, a way of teaching the offender to be good:

> I remember a long time ago when I was a young boy, when I started getting a little bad, my late grandmother, Mabel York, used to send me out to go and get a red willow switch for punishment. So, trying to be a good boy, I would go out and try to find the best looking one. I would bring it back to her and ask her if it was ok. She would say "Yes," then she proceeded to tap you on your butt or the back of your legs. I tell you she never hit you hard, but it sure made you jump every time she tapped you with it.
>
> Now all this time later, I think about it and chuckle because I ask myself why did I have to go and get my own medicine. Well, I guess if I didn't listen to her, then it might have been worse and it also probably means I didn't respect her by not listening to her. So I guess you could say that I didn't turn out so bad. When I mention this to my Aunt Fran and Uncle Don, we sure have a good laugh. She was a great Lady. (*The Georgina Island Storytelling Project*, 2006, p. 8)

For an Aboriginal person to be a teacher was rare for many years after Lorenzo Big Canoe taught. In the annual report for 1960, there were only 116 Aboriginal teachers across all of Canada, making up a meagre 8.9 percent of the population of teachers that were working with Aboriginal children at that time (Jones, 1960, p. 56).

When Lorenzo Big Canoe became chief in 1947, he had strong views as to how the Georgina Island day school should be run. These he communicated to a federal Special Joint Committee that year. He stated that he desired that

> the system of using missionary teachers be abolished. We would like to see our day school system supervised by a school board, as in white communities, so that a properly qualified teacher will always get the appointment [as reported in the *Truth and Reconciliation Commission of Canada*, vol. 1, part 2, p. 30].

His son Albert, when interviewed in 2016, reflected his father's view in talking about the long history of "preacher teachers" that were hired to teach on Georgina Island. Not a few were Methodist ministers. Even when they weren't, religion was still a strong influence on what was taught. Robert Moyes, for example, the teacher during the 1880s, was not a preacher by profession, but:

> He dedicates his time on Sunday to the spiritual improvement of Indians, as he does through the week to their social, intellectual, and moral advancement. (Fotheringham, 1886, p. 127)

The Big Canoes Escape Residential School
(From a Story Told by Andrew Big Canoe, 2017)

The plan was to have the Big Canoe brothers, Andrew and Albert, go to the Mohawk Institute residential school in Brantford, the infamous "Mushhole" as the students called it. Their parents came with them to see what the conditions were at the school. They were shown a nice bedroom that they were told would be where the boys would stay. They were told about students being well-fed, with roast beef and such.

Lorenzo Big Canoe and Family

After the parents left, the boys got a hard dose of reality. They were taken to the dormitories where they would be sleeping with a lot of other boys. They had toast and porridge (the mush) for breakfast every morning, while they could see that the people who worked there had eggs and bacon and other nutritious and tasty foods.

So after two weeks, Andrew Big Canoe escaped. He would soon be followed by his brother. The latter was done through the help of their father Lorenzo Big Canoe. He was well-known and was respected even in federal government circles. So when he declared that his boys were not going to go to such a horrible place, people in power listened. This is how the Big Canoe boys were able to escape from residential school.

Facing Hard Educational Choices

For years, once children graduated from the day school on Georgina Island, the students, their parents, and families faced some hard choices. The children could board with family, friends, or paid strangers on the mainland, and go to a school in the Sutton area. There were residential schools far away, but few wanted to go that route. Other options involved quitting school and going to work.

RICHARD CHARLES—JOURNAL—1998 (BORN AUGUST 19, 1935)

I went to school when I was seven years old. Lorenzo, my neighbour, was my first teacher. There was an old school there, on the island, built in 1885, I think. The school was torn down about forty years ago. I think it was called Georgina Island Indian Day School. Lorenzo taught me to about grade 3 or 4, then my teacher was Mr. Frank Joblin. He was about 75 years old. He used to come to our place every Sunday night, with his wife Maude, to listen to the radio; Charlie McCarthy and Ed Sullivan… My last teacher on the island was Mr. Harris, for one or two years…

When I was 13, I moved up to high school. My father moved to Jackson's Point. You had to be on the mainland to get to school.

LEONARD PORTE (SARGE)—OCTOBER 25, 2014 (BORN 1942)

I remember starting school on the island, I was six years old in 1948, in grade one. I only spoke Ojibway, but I had to learn English. It was very hard. The teacher Mr. Lowen was mean and wasn't like a teacher. He was more like a preacher. He hit us, and one day, he hit my sister Glenda. So my friend Lam Charles put a snake in his desk…

As a teenager, I was told and so were the other young men on island, that we had to go to residential school. Our parents would not have this. So I ran away to Acton to find work.

Today education on Georgina Island is quite different from what students experienced in schools of the past. *Waabgon Gamig* ('Blossoming House') is a band-operated day school, with students from junior kindergarten to grade six. It has two classrooms, and uses the island as an outdoor education facility. Teacher Tanya Leary introduces her presentation about her school, specifically the Mother Earth Mentorship program, in the following way:

Waabgon Gamig

> Imagine a teacher who drives across a frozen lake to get to work. Imagine a teacher who brings owl puke and a dead porcupine to school to use in her critical inquiry lesson. Imagine a school with only 23 students and five staff on a remote island that doubles as an outdoor classroom. Although the school follows the Ontario Elementary Curriculum, it has several features which clearly mark it as a culturally-focused school. The emphasis on the environment and traditional culture, and teaching about and frequent use of the language of the people show this.

Success in Education for Georgina Islanders

In the last few decades, Georgina Islanders have done well in the education system. The introduction of a reliable, regular ferry meant that the commute to school on the mainland no longer required students to stay on the mainland during the school year. On any school day that you are on the island waiting for the always busy weekday 3:30 p.m. ferry to go to the mainland, you can see a small group of pre-teens and teenagers getting off the ferry and going home. The stories they will someday tell their children and grandchildren about their commute to school (except possibly for tales of the Scoot—see the chapter on "The Crossing"—that carries passengers in the winter) will be quite different from those told by their grandparents.

The success of the Georgina Islanders in education was neatly summed up by elder Barb McDonald when she said that "We've got doctors, lawyers and Indian Chiefs." She could add nurses, teachers, and other educated professionals to that list.

Dr. John R. Big Canoe

An example of the former was Dr. John R. Big Canoe. He lost his parents when he was quite young, and lived most of his life off reserve, in both Ontario and Quebec. Still, despite this separation from the community, when he decided to become a doctor, the band agreed to pay for his medical school tuition. He went to Quebec to get his initial medical training, graduating from the University of Montreal in 1992. He did his post-graduate work at the University of Toronto, becoming a full-fledged doctor in 1994 at age 33. He was talented and would easily have made a good living as a doctor in the big city. But he wanted to pay the community back for supporting his way through medical school, and he wanted his children to be raised in the traditions of his people. He became the first doctor to live on the island so that the people had ready access to medical services in an emergency, something they appreciated. Dr. Big Canoe worked at the Georgina Medical Clinic on the mainland. For his first months as a doctor, he rowed to work and back again, as he was athletic and he wanted to experience the traditional Georgina Island contact with the surrounding waters. Unfortunately, like a number of the people before and after him, he died one day (November 9, 1994) in making the crossing. The community's loss was great.

DR. JOHN BIGCANOE

But his story carries on in a number of ways, including scholarships named after him. In 2014, award-winning Dr. Darlene Kelly, a Cree doctor who, like Dr. John Big Canoe, was the first in her community to achieve that status, talked about how Dr. John Big Canoe was a role model for her:

> He told me his story and how he persevered to get in, study well and graduate from medical school. He told me not to give up and not to let them say that you are not good enough… I now repeat his message when I speak to youth. (*The Nation*, 2014)

On the island, Dr. John Lane, off of the main road of Joseph Snake Trail, is named after him.

Lawyers

In the dark past of Aboriginal people and through the restrictive power of the Indian Act (specifically section 141, instituted in 1927), bands were not permitted to hire non-Aboriginal lawyers to argue their land claims. And if status Indians went to law school, they would be forced to renounce their status, and become enfranchised, giving up their rights. That changed in 1951. The first status Indian Aboriginal lawyer was Alberta Cree William Wuttunee, who became a lawyer in 1954. The first female status Indian Aboriginal lawyer was a Mohawk woman, Roberta Jamieson, who graduated in 1976. Georgina Island has raised lawyers, specifically Duncan McCue and Christa Big Canoe.

Duncan McCue was called to the bar in 1998, but heard a louder voice coming from CBC, where he has become an award-winning radio and television journalist. He was the host of CBC Radio's popular show *Cross Country Checkup*. Later he was the host of *Helluva Story* on CBC One, and produced an eight-part podcast on residential schools for CBC podcasts. It is called "Kuper Island," named after an infamous residential school in British Columbia with a high death rate. As an author he has written a textbook, *Decolonizing Journalism: A Guide to Reporting in Indigenous Communities*, and *The Shoe Boy*, a recounting of a summer he spent with a Cree family in northern Quebec as a teenager.

Then there is Christa Big Canoe. She speaks of herself on LinkedIn as follows:

> As a First Nation woman, mother and lawyer, I aspire to increase access to justice for Aboriginal people. I have actively participated in First Nation and Aboriginal community throughout my life. I took a two and a half year leave in 2017 from Aboriginal Legal Services to be senior legal counsel and then Lead Commission Counsel for the National Inquiry in to Missing and Murdered Indigenous Women and Girls. I have been back at Aboriginal Legal Services since July 2019. I have previously been Policy Counsel for Legal Aid Ontario and the lead on the organization's province-wide Aboriginal Justice Strategy. I also am passionate about First Nation children and women's rights, the right to equal access to education and care. (https/ca.linkedin.com/in/christa-big-canoe-219a092b)

Georgina Island Teachers

There are teachers from Georgina Island at all levels of education from preschool through elementary school and high school to college and university. Kim Big Canoe heads the Niigaan-Naabiwag ('Looking Ahead') Child Care Centre on the island.

Snake Island's Dr. Harvey McCue at 25 graduated from Trent University with a B.A. in sociology in 1969. But it hadn't been an easy path for him. He had first enrolled at Laurentian University in Sudbury, and it had proved difficult: "I barely got through... there was a lot of racism... It was a huge shock to me. I really didn't have the skills to cope adequately with it" (Pellinger, 2014).

After McCue graduated from Trent University, the president of the university, Thomas Symons, asked to speak with him, and together they founded the first department of Native Studies in Canada in 1971. Shortly afterwards he published under the name Waubageshig,[28] meaning White Sky and referring to the colour of the sky before the sun rises. It was the first book in Canada edited by an Aboriginal person and containing essays by Aboriginal people: *The Only Good Indian: Essays by Canadian Indians* (1974). In 1983, he moved on to work for the Cree School Board in Northern Quebec, the first Aboriginal-controlled provincial school board in Canada. By 1988, he took on the federal government in their own house, first serving as Director of Policy and Research within the education branch, two years later becoming the Director General of that branch, the first Aboriginal person to do so. From there he became the Executive Director of the innovative Mi'kmaq Education Authority, until he retired to do consulting work in 1995.

Shelley Charles, like the previous two Georgina Islanders, is a success in mainstream education, with an M.A. in Indigenous Philosophy, and was for years the Indigenous Advisor and Dean of Indigenous Education and Engagement at Humber College, where she had been instrumental in creating a strong Aboriginal presence. Like the above-mentioned Georgina Islanders, she combines a deep understanding of traditional Anishinaabe education as a third degree Midewiwin and member of the *Maazhi gnoozhe* or Fish Clan, educated and educating in the knowledge of Indigenous and mainstream society—the best of both worlds. That phrase sums up well the approach to education of the Chippewas of Georgina Island.

---

28. It is also the name of Waubegeshig Rice, a prolific Anishinaabe author.

Cynthia Wesley-Esquimaux

The previously mentioned Cynthia Wesley-Esquimaux has been a leading figure in Canada in what she calls the "Indigenizing" of universities. Her own educational path was not an easy or smooth one. She has described it as follows:

> I was one of those indigenous students who dropped out of school. I had completed grade 9 and maybe had gone into grade 10. There was so much racism at the time. It seemed like there was never an end to being called names or being centred out as being the only Native student in the class. I dropped out. I went to work, and four years later I moved to Palm Springs, California for five years. While I was in California I went back to school. I actually graduated from Palm Springs High. After that, I went to the College of the Desert, into the associative arts program. And I thought: I can do this. This is not as hard as I thought.
>
> I applied to U of T. I was the only Native student at that time out in [the] Scarborough [campus] until another Native student started, but he didn't graduate. While I was there I got married, and I got pregnant with twins. It was pretty challenging.
>
> Later, I found I did not have the grades that were necessary to get into graduate school, so I just went and argued with them... I said, "You have to let me in because I'm Native, and because things are shifting. We need to be retrained and educated, and I need that graduate degree."
>
> They let me in. (University of Toronto Scarborough Campus, 2021)

She wanted to do her research on the historic trauma of the effect of the residential schools, not just on the Indigenous students, but their children and grandchildren as well:

> I was [pursuing work on] historic trauma. They said, "We don't know what that is. There's nothing in the literature. You have to do something that has been done." I said, "Well then, let's put it in the literature."

Her own life history led her to investigate the subject of historic trauma. Her parents between them survived 20 years of Indian Residential Schools

(IRS). Raised in an environment of IRS survivor binge drinking, sexual and domestic violence and erratic care and support, she understood what it meant to navigate family and community chaos. Before she had dropped out of high school she had experienced relatively short stints in Toronto's Juvenile Hall and Children's Aid before the age of 16.

She received her M.A. in 1998, her Ph.D. in 2004. From there she has pursued a successful career in university education, not just of the students, but more informally teaching professors and administrators as well. This has included her becoming in 2013 the Vice Provost for Indigenous Initiatives at Lakehead and in 2016 the inaugural Indigenous Chair in Truth and Reconciliation in Canada there as well, followed by becoming the Chair of the Governing Circle for the National Centre for Truth and Reconciliation at the University of Manitoba, doing similar work as well at her alma mater of the University of Toronto.

A recent part of her promotion of "indigenizing" the universities has involved promoting the full-time hiring of Elders as permanent staff, not just people called in once a year to give a lecture. She learned of the wisdom of Elders from her grandfather Lorenzo Big Canoe.

CHAPTER SIX

Black Ash Baskets, Fancy Work, and Woodwork

In 1907, John Yates, the Indian Agent at the time, commented in the *Annual Report of the Department of Indian Affairs* on the skilled crafting of the women of Georgina Island, and how the baskets were exchanged for other goods, and also purchased: "The women make baskets and fancy-work. There is ready sale and good prices for all they make" (Yates, 1907, p. 52).

The baskets were made out of black ash, and the "fancy-work" usually involved dyed porcupine quills or beads stitched in creative patterns on birch bark. And the "ready sale" often involved the women travelling long distances in summer to the mainland where the cottagers and other tourists were. The women crafters often took with them their children and husbands. The men would often earn money during this travelling through guiding fishing trips, and selling fish and wooden handicrafts of their own.

People from near and far on the mainland would even make a special trip to the island specifically to buy samples of this beautiful work. In 1885, Indian agent J. R. Stevenson remarked in the *Annual Report of the Department of Indian Affairs*: "Many of my friends come from distant parts of the country to visit the island, and always make some purchases of fancy work to carry home with them, and on many occasions have sent the artwork to England" (Stevenson, 1885, p. 78).

Victoria Harbour is a community on the south shore of Georgian Bay, east of Midland. This photograph shows a family that travelled there, probably to sell baskets.

The black ash baskets, quillwork, objects made of sweetgrass, and birchbark were a medium of contact and exchange between the Georgina Islanders and the mainlanders.

Lillian Dallimore, a longtime resident and local historian of the Sandy Cove area of Innisfil, north and west of Snake Island, by the western shores of Lake Simcoe, reminisced in 1984 in the *Historical Review* of the *Innisfil Historical Society* about members of the Big Sail family who had moved in nearby, especially remarking on the black ash baskets that the family made:

> The family was known as Big Sails, and I remember Paul, Charlotte and Emily bringing all kinds of beautifully decorated baskets, small boats, clothes hampers, and handker-chief boxes. They were very clever with sweet grasses, porcupine quills, fine beadwork and dyes. The dyes they made from the sumac tree and various berries. The farmwives purchased their wares by trading food products for them. (Dallimore, 1984, p. 220)

Left: The Big Sails of Sandy Cove and their Baskets.

Below left: Men's wood work: Cedar chairs. Georgina Island families including the Ashquabes and Portes would set up, build and sell furniture at Jackson's Point and Sibbald's Point.

Men's Work

As you will read shortly, men were traditionally involved with the hard physical labour of the first stages of making black ash baskets. They were also involved with crafting many objects out of wood for home use, barter, or sale: fish decoys (see the "Going Fishing" chapter), axe-handles, oars, paddles, rice beaters (see picture in "The Crossing"), canoes, chairs and other furniture, sleighs (for carrying people, supplies and articles

A People of Stories

for sale in the winter), whiffletrees (the horizontal wooden bars just in front of a horse-drawn plough) and buildings, both log cottages and frame houses and barns, for themselves and for non-Indigenous mainlanders.

Right: William (Bill) Ashquabe, Birchbark wigwam and canoes (created in 1919). http://www.georginaisland.com.php72-37. lan3-1.websitetestlink.com/artifact/birch-bark-canoes-and-teepee/

Right: Carved by Phillip Ashquabe. https://georginaisland.com/artifact/wooden-carved-box/ (The Georgina Island Storytelling Project)

Black Ash Baskets: It Takes a Family to Make a Basket

Baskets made out of black ash (*aagimaak* or *wiisgaak*)[29] have long been a tradition of the Anishinaabe people, and of their Mi'kmaq and Abenaki cousins in the eastern provinces as well. Their use of this tree shows that the people had long ago learned that, unique among trees, the black ash has seasonal growth rings that are not as firmly connected to each other as is the case with other trees. This makes it easier to separate the layers for the construction of baskets from splints made of the layers. But keep in mind that easier does not mean "easy." Every step in the process requires hard work and skill, from women, men and children. It takes a family to make a black ash basket.

First the black ash trees are found and felled. Then the bark is removed. The trunk that remains is kept moist through soaking so that the wood is more flexible and less likely to crack when it is being worked. Then the men (and some women) do the heavy work. They pound the trunk with the back

---

29. In the 19th century it was recorded that there were two more Aanishinaabemowin names for what appear to be kinds of ash trees: *gawâkomij* and *papagimak* (Baraga, 1992, p. 18).

of an axe until the rings are separated. This does not take a short time. Some sort of cleaver is then used to pry the rings apart. They are then cut into splints. The splints are kept moist and they are planed so that they they can be worked. Some of the splints are cut into thinner strips to be used to bind the thicker ones. Women then dye some of the splints to make some pretty fancy baskets. As you see from the pictures, not all black ash baskets are the same. The baskets have been used to carry different things, and the creativity of makers has made for different styles as well. It was not uncommon for styles of baskets to be passed down from mothers and grandmothers to daughters and granddaughters.

In the reports of the various Indian agents who worked with the Chippewa of Georgina Island in the late nineteenth century and early twentieth century, a regular positively reported item was mention of the black ash baskets and how they earned money for the people of Georgina Island. The reports several times mentioned that there was a good market for the baskets, especially as they were often used for carrying apples and other fruits and vegetables and that the baskets fetched a decent price.

In 1889, there was special mention of how the women of the community had made $100 from selling these baskets to people on the mainland, enough to pay for the church organ. On Sundays they could hear the benefit from the hard work that they and their families had engaged in.

As you will read in the words of Richard Charles below, black ash basket making was a family affair, with at least three generations (possibly four) having a part to play before the final product was available for sale.

RICHARD CHARLES, 1998 JOURNAL

Starting when I was about five or six, my mother and father used to make and sell baskets out of black ash trees from our woodlands. My father used to get the black ash and then we used to pound it with the back of the axe until strips came loose. They had to be a certain thickness too. We used to have an old fellow, named Roger Ashquaabe, who helped to pound the black ash... My mother used to get a knife and peel it to a certain thickness and she'd run it through some sort of sharp thing to shred it to a certain width. Then she dyed the black ash with a special dye from the drug stores. My mother used to weave the baskets. I did a few too. I used to weave the little candy baskets and got about 50 cents to a dollar for each one. After she made so many, she and my dad and Viola Johnson used to take them to Beaverton by boat to sell them along the way. They had to stop on the way sometimes because the water got so rough. The basket business was filling orders for cottagers along the waterway. It'd take about a day to make a big hamper basket, or two or three small baskets. You could weave about five or six baskets from a single tree. Mom did this weaving only in the summertime. She also made model birch bark canoes and covered jewelry cases with quillwork woven on the top in different designs.

And ash baskets were part of the barter system in the community, where work and goods get traded but no money changed hands. (Charles, 1998)

The Charles family also engaged in the collecting and processing of maple syrup:

My dad had about 50 acres of wild land. From it we would get our trees, but also gathered sap in the spring to make our own maple syrup. I was about 10 or 12 years old when I started helping my dad gather the sap. There were about 75 to 100 maple trees. We just made it for ourselves and used to give some of it away to family and neighbours

We used to make maple syrup candy too. We boiled the sap until it got goey, then pound it into moulds. (Charles, 1998)

Charles (Charlie) Warren
(July 24, 2013—Interview by Suzanne Howes and Leah Atkinson)

My grandfather used to get the ash, and old Roger Ashquabe used to come and pound the ash ... and he'd get a free meal out of it or whatever. Then during the late fall and winter, that's when you started making baskets. And my grandmother and my grandfather made these baskets. Everybody had a share in it, everybody, our family wasn't the only one. Everybody else on the whole island did the same thing, and then came spring, which I hated, my grandmother would use me as her donkey. She would wash me and give me a good scrubbing and everything. I hated it and carried the damn baskets, and they make a trade for some money and some clothes. My grandmother always wanted clothes more than anything else 'cause she could make clothes for all of us. So it was quite a thing, and you would go across in the rowboat, my grandfather would go and work and we could go and sell baskets.

You went across wherever you lived. And if it was rough, then you didn't go over. It was always a day that it was calm. And we'd come back the same day, and if I was lucky we'd get an ice cream cone.

BEATRICE MCCUE (JULY 17, 2002—INTERVIEWER SHERI TAYLOR):
TRAVELLING WITH QUILLWORK AND BASKETS

Black ash. My uncle pounded the ash. There was always ash around the house when I was growing up at my Grans because she did all the basketwork. She did all kinds. I still have some of her work. I still have some baskets that my mom made.

But the quillwork I learned as a little kid because we used to go to Port Carling, my mom and I. She worked her way making quillwork for the people she used to live with, and I used to play with all the kids there and kids from Gibson reserve, Mohawks, and the kids from Rama. But we travelled all over. We used to travel by canoe. There would be five canoes that would leave Longford in about June. Then we would camp at Sparrow Lake. We would set up tents and there was always one woman who looked after the kids while the women went selling baskets and the men did guiding for fishing. Oh my life was really… I think I should write a story about it, because I've got so many things I could tell about my life. (McCue, 2002)

Selling the Baskets

It wasn't just in the making of the baskets that the women of Georgina Island showed their ingenuity and determination. They also had to sell them, find a market for them on the mainland. This often involved a lot of travel around the area. Whole families would often go together in this enteprise.

DELORES CHARLES (INTERVIEW)

Delores: Lil McCue? She[30] used to visit her a lot and … I got a picture of her sitting, making baskets. She used to make baskets. That's why Mom used to go over there, I guess.

---

30. Delores Charles' mother.

Interviewer: And did they go to Port Carling?
Delores: Port Carling. Mom used to say they used to go sell.
Interviewer: Even quill work, eh?
Delores: Mmmmhmm. I can still see them.
Interviewer: They didn't come back until everything was sold.
Delores: Yuh. And Don used to tell me he went with his mom. Remember going to sell baskets.
Interviewer: Who was his mom?
Delores: Mabel York. When she was a kid, she'd take them to the Jackson's Point, I guess go down there and sell their baskets. Can you imagine how much those baskets are worth now?
Interviewer: Ya, eh?
Delores: Holy. That's real art. You know, make the designs on there and stuff. Man. I wonder what they got. I wonder if they bartered for food or just, whatever, eh? Now that's a dying art. The guys would get the black ash. That was their duty. And then they would pound it and then they would strip it. Get it all ready for the women. And then they… I just remember them going "shweesh." The noise, "shweesh." Making it, like with the knife. (shweesh). Making big long strands. (heh!) Making them soft and making the baskets.

Mavis Trivett—Ash Baskets (interview, n.d.)

This is what—I would have been like, five—because my grandpa died at an early age—when I was really young. But I remember sitting out when he'd do the ash pounding. When they went to pick the logs, they'd always go out with the horses and you know, he'd bring in so many. So many—he never brought in a lot because he just took what they needed. And, I'd be sitting on an old anvil, and sitting there watching him. They'd soak it. I can't remember how long they soaked—they'd just soak it in the water. Like, he'd probably take it down to the lake. They'd soak it in there tied up, and soak it in the water. And he'd bring it up—and he'd be just pounding, eh? He—I'd watch him and he'd be going from … as he'd be pounding all the way down the end, eh. He'd turn the log and then he'd pound and then he'd strip it and I just get in trouble because when he'd strip them—like, he'd strip about a four-inch strip and I'd sit there and I'd get a hold of one and I'd peel it… He'd be pounding on the ash and I'd just sit and watch.

How Do You Get Quills?

You could not buy porcupine quills in a store, so Georgina Island women had to be ever diligent in acquiring them however they could. Elder Susan Hoeg used to carry a pair of pliers with her when she was in a car, just in case there was a reasonably fresh porcupine roadkill on the side of the road. She should have had a bumper sticker on her car declaring, "This car brakes for porcupine quills." Others on the island would surely have understood.

Below: Quill basket (left). Collection of crafts (centre and right).

CHAPTER SEVEN

Going Fishing

Fishing Rights

The fishing rights the people correctly believed were theirs by treaty had to be fought for. William Plummer, Visiting Superintendent and Commissioner of Indian Affairs (1876–1881), had heard criticism from the people of Georgina Island about the $30 licensing fee imposed by the Department of Marine and Fisheries that community members had to pay for fishing the waters around their home islands. In 1878, he wrote to the federal minister that:

> There should be set apart for these Indians, the water around the two small islands on which they reside, namely Georgina and Snake Islands in Lake Simcoe for home use only. The Fishery Overseer at Barrie has charged these Indians $30 a year for the privilege of fishing around Georgina Island which is considered by all to be great hardship, but to which they have been compelled to submit in order to keep away a very undesirable class of white men who are in the habit of bringing whiskey and committing many worse abominations. (Blair, 2008, p. 66)

W.E. Whitcher, federal Deputy Commissioner of Marine and Fisheries, condemned Plummer for his "illegal notions" and "false advice."

When local Fishery Overseer Col. Alex Mckenzie agreed to acknowledge the traditional rights of the people of Georgina Island to fish around the islands, and had their agreement submitted to the Marine and Fisheries in 1888, along with a request that they have their license fee refunded, this was denied in the name of "the threatened destruction of fish in the above-named waters" because of the people's practice of netting fish (something they had done for centuries without negatively affecting the fish population). The Deputy Minister felt that non-Aboriginal fishers would make a "well-founded complaint" about the "special favour" (i.e., treaty rights) granted the people (Blair, 2008, p. 72).

A fishing license was granted to Noah Snake "for the Indians" in May 1875 by Alex McKenzie, Fishing Overseer for the Department of Marine and Fisheries.

The Georgina Island fishery was very important to the people, not just for food but also for income. In 1883, it was reckoned by the Indian Agent that the 135 people of the community caught $300 worth of fish (*Annual Report of the Department of Indian Affairs*, 1883, p. 20). During this time, earning such an income by fishing "for trade or barter" was contested by the government if it involved treaty rights. Even after the Williams Treaties negotiations of 1923 (see below), the fishing rights of the people were not clearly defined by the government.

But fishing for income continued, despite resistance from the federal government. Some elders living today have spoken about lake whitefish selling for five cents a pound during their lifetime, with whitefish in such quantity that island families could earn important dollars from the sale of fish, often made by going from door-to-door on the mainland. This brought in funds for buying necessary goods in the stores there. Everybody in the area benefited.

The Georgina Island tradition of catching whitefish and selling them to people on the mainland continued into at least the 1950s. During much of that time, there was more than a small chance that people eating a whitefish in a restaurant in Toronto were consuming a fish sold to the restaurant owners by a merchant who bought the fish from someone from Georgina Island who had caught it in Lake Simcoe.

Lake Simcoe Fish and Their Names

Here are the *Anishinaabemowin* names for some of the most important fish in Lake Simcoe. Elder Barbara McDonald supplied these names. The scientific species name for the lake trout, *namaycush*, is derived from the term that Georgina Islanders have long used for this fish. The -(a)g ending for these names is the plural.

Gaa(wag)	walleye (pickerel)
Gnoozhe(g)	pike
Maazhi gnoozhe ('big pike')	muskellunge (muskie)
Goodaashiinh(ag)	crappie
Kweis(ag)	lake herring or cisco
Nmegos(ag)	lake trout
Saawe(g)	perch
Shigan(ag)	bass
Tikmeg(wag)	lake whitefish

Barbara McDonald

Winter Fishing
Fish Decoys: Okeau

(This section is adapted in part from *Our Fishing Story* [2013]. The Georgina Island member who provided this information is not identified.)

In winters of years gone past, when holes were drilled in the ice, lake trout were caught using a carved wooden fish decoy or *okeau*. Woods used included basswood, leatherwood (a bush with yellow flowers), pine, and cedar. These fish-decoys would resemble a small lake herring (cisco) or other small fish species that lived in the waters of Lake Simcoe.

During the construction of the fish decoy, the stomach of the false wooden fish was hollowed out to allow for melted lead to be poured inside it. The added weight allowed it to sink. The decoys were also equipped with tin fins and a tin tail. Tails on the okeau would be curved, causing the decoy to swim in a circle at it was raised and lowered through the water—the "jigging" of the decoy. To the fish, it would look like a smaller fish was swimming in front of them.

The okeau would traditionally be used with spears (*anit*) in shallow waters (about two metres), with the okeau luring the fish to the ice hole to be speared.

The earliest written account of Anishinaabe using fish decoys when ice fishing was recorded by the fur trader Alexander Henry the Elder, sometime during the early 1760s, in the area near where the city of Sault Ste. Marie is now.

In order to spear the trout under the ice, holes [were] first cut of two yards in circumference, cabins of about two feet in height built over them of small branches of trees and these are further covered with skins so as to wholly exclude the light. The design and result of this contrivance is, to render it practicable to discern objects in the water at a very considerable depth; for the reflection of the light from the water gives that element an opaque appearance, and hides all objects from the eye, at a small distance beneath its surface.

A spearhead of iron is fastened on a pole, of about ten feet in length. This instrument is lowered into the water; and the fisherman, lying upon his belly, with his head under the cabin or cover and therefore over the hole, lets down a figure of a fish in wood, and filled with lead. Round the middle of the fish [decoy], is tied a small packthread; and, when at the depth of ten fathom, where it is intended to be employed, it is made, by drawing the string and by the simultaneous pressure of the water, to move forward and after the manner of a real fish.

Trout and other large fish, deceived by its resemblance, spring toward it to seize it; but, by a dextrous jerk of the string, it is instantly take[n] from their reach. The decoy is now drawn near to the surface; and the fish takes some time to renew the attack, during which, the spear is raised and held conveniently for striking. On the return of the fish, the spear is plunged into its back; and, the spear being barbed, it is easily drawn out of the water (Henry, 1809, pp. 64–5).

Closer to Georgina Island, Thomas Need wrote in 1833 of people from the Curve Lake First Nation fishing in his *Six Years in the Bush: Extracts from the Journal of a Settler in Upper Canada:1832–1838*:

We observed some forty or fifty of them in their picturesque gypsy-

like tents, watch for fish. They will stand many hours together over a hole in the ice, darkened by blankets, with a fish-spear in one hand, and a wooden decoy fish attached to a line in the other waiting for a muskelonge or pike which they strike with almost unerring certainty…
In this way, a skillful fisherman will catch 50 to 200 lbs. weight of fish in a day. (Need, 1833, p. 44–5)

With the introduction of tin cans to North America early in the nineteenth century, tin fins were added to the *okeau*, enabling it to more freely dance in front of the intended target fish.

Settlers in the Lake Simcoe area who fished for food and for sport learned about *okeau* from the people of Georgina Island. They then added new materials and designs to the traditional Anishinaabe fish-decoys. Winter spearing of fish became a common and successful practice in the Lake Simcoe area. From 1907, when licenses were first required for spearing fish, until 1941, when spearing fish was banned, it was estimated that some 500,000 pounds of fish were taken in this manner.

Fish huts in which fishermen employed hooks, lines, and rods took over during the winter fishing. By 1948, there were 1,450 registered ice fishing huts on the lake. Now Lake Simcoe is generally referred to as the most heavily fished inland lake in Ontario. It got to a state where the numbers of the once plentiful cisco were so low in the lake that from 2001 to 2015 fishing for them was banned completely. In 2024 the limit was two.

Spring Fishing

In the spring, lake trout and whitefish in the past could (and today still can) be found in shallow waters of the lake as well as up the creeks of Georgina Island. Traditionally, the fishing was easy, and it was good to get fresh fish for a change after a long hard winter of salted fish. The combination of fresh fish, fry bread, and newly tapped and simmered maple syrup made for good spring eating.

Lake Simcoe was stocked with rainbow smelt in the early 1960s. This was not a good idea as they are now considered an invasive species, as, among other faults, they eat the young of fish native to the lake. Rainbow smelt are not native to the lake. As newcomers, they have no traditional Anishinaabemowin name. Rainbow smelt would, from the 1960s, be caught in large numbers using nets of all kinds and buckets when the fish spawned in April, in the creeks and in the shallows. From there they are either sold or eaten by those who caught them.

Suckers, which are native to Lake Simcoe, would also be caught at this time as they would traditionally swim up the streams of Georgina Island. This important food fish would be canned for the people's own use later in the year. The English word for the fish is misleadingly negative. It was traditionally well-respected by the Chippewas of Georgina Island. In fact, the term for February for many Anishinaabe people in Ontario is *Namebini Giizis* or Sucker Moon, based on the word *namebin* for sucker. Some Anishinaabe peoples belong to the Sucker Clan, another sign of great respect for this fish.

The Fall Fish

In the fall, three significant fish spawn. Lake trout generally spawn around Thanksgiving. They are followed shortly afterwards by lake whitefish, afterward by cisco. Traditionally, they were often so plentiful that they could be caught in buckets.

Of course, with the large number of fish caught there would come a fish feast on Georgina Island. Here is one story about that feast. Andrew Big Canoe, an elder well-known for his storytelling, speaks here of the traditional fish feast in the fall:

> One thing I remember is we used to have a big fish feast in the fall in October when the trout would come in and the ladies over here would put on a big meal on a Sunday and what it was called was a Sunday church celebration. And the men would go net fish, then they'd clean all the fish and the ladies would cook 'em all up with all the potatoes and vegetables, people would come from Rama and Curve Lake, Scugog, Alderville, people from Christian Island. Quite a few people would come, and in those days they had to come over in a row boat somebody would go over and bring three or four people at a time. We'd get quite a big crowd here and people would bunk in with someone. We didn't have a motel or anything over here. If they had relatives they stay with them. I remember people staying here with us, ya know if ya had a couch or an old mattress some people would bring sleeping bags and sleep on the floor. It was quite an event, no drinking and they would have a big church service…

Plus fish, fish was plentiful, lots of fish. There was no limit on how many whitefish you could catch or trout until the mid-'60's, early '70's, the people from the mainland started to come fishing and they were taking them by the hundreds of thousands of pounds so the ministry stepped in. That's why we have a limit on the fish now. So they were going to clean the lake out if we didn't stop them. Our people would go out fishing and throw a net out and maybe enough fish to feed us for a month and we'd go around in the spring time spearing, everything we had we'd either salt or dry. When we got hydro here in the sixties, fifties, maybe it was the fifties, we started buying freezers so we started to freeze our fish and stuff. But that's all gone now, you can't fish, you can't even hunt. We can hunt over here but nowhere else. And fishing, I'm exempt from it now because I'm over 65, but you have to get a license to fish on the lake. Which isn't right for our people we've fished here for over thousands of years ... we lived good. (Andrew Big Canoe interview, 2014).

Charlie Warren and the Perils of Eating Fish

Not everybody liked the plentiful fish that would be available throughout the year. In an interview with Charles Warren he made that point very clear:

We had fish, fish, fish. That's the reason I don't like fish.

My grandmother would cook fish. She'd say, "Go out and catch some fish for supper," and she meant it. You'd only be gone for 10, 15 minutes, you'd get what, 20 or something, nice big bass and so on. You were always able to get white fish and trout. My grandfather would go from here, go to work in Jackson's Point and he'd catch fish, trout on the way over and he'd sell them in Jackson's Point and it was all extra money.

My grandmother knew how to cook and my grandmother never wasted a damned thing... There were several ways my grandmother cooked fish. She boiled some and she roasted some ... and she also baked white fish or trout, mostly trout.

And they also fried trout, always had a lot of pork fat. Every time, they killed a pig in the fall, one or two they'd render up all the fat on the pig and that's what was used for everything. Even if you were going to make a sandwich, you had a piece of bread that your grandma made, cut that open and put the pork fat on it, and salt and pepper and lots of pepper and that's the way it was done.

But with the fish, there was so many ways that you could cook. There was no particular one way. It was according to who would do the cooking.

We used to wrap them, and cook them in coals, with big leaves, whatever was around

I don't know what kind of leaves they used, but you know, that's what they used to do. They'd mix each batch with salt on it, and it was rubbed in so it would cover every part of the fish. There'd be salt on the bottom. Each layer would have salt and on the top there would be salt as well. They put the lid back on and they would leave it for the winter. One at a time, they never took them all out, because they weren't even spoiled when you opened them up. But they'd already be in the brine and then you had to soak them over night and keep changing the water until you were ready to cook them because they had a lot of salt in them. And sometimes they'd kill ye ... but anyway, you'd go to the bathroom with the runs. (Laughs)

Ron Charles Interview

Ron Charles: The trout would come in first. Just a little bit after Thanksgiving. Sometimes right on Thanksgiving. Around Thanksgiving. Because we used to have a fish fry here every fall. Trout right on Thanksgiving.
Interviewer: Who would do the fish fry?
Ron Charles: All the ladies in that old church there, where they used to have the wood stove. They used to cook them on the wood stove in that old hall. But the wood stoves and that... it was a long time ago. I was probably—maybe fifteen? Sixteen? Whenever they came in, they could have trout first, and their own Thanksgiving and then they'd be in for two or three weeks and then they'd go out, and then the white fishers would come in around the first of November, or first week in November—and they'd be—for a couple of weeks and then they'd have white fish.
Interviewer: How did the ladies prepare it?
Ron Charles: Mostly fried.
Interviewer: And then what else? Did everyone bring dishes?
Ron Charles: Ya. Kind of a potluck. Well... ya, but they used to cook everything there too. Vegetables. I don't remember too much corn being

served back then. There probably was. They'd have rolls and that. Homemade bread, they used to have. Pies. Big dinners. Fish fries.

Interviewer: Did a lot of people have their own gardens?

Ron Charles: Yep.

Interviewer: And they just brought food?

Ron Charles

Ron Charles: Ya, everyone had their own garden. And after white fish came in, just before freeze-up, the herring would come in and you'd get them.

Leonard Porte on Fishing

I love to fish and always gave my first away to the community. We all relied on the lake fish for our main food. No money was exchanged for this. The lake had lots of fish, not like today. The fish now tastes off, and now I only eat fish in the spring.

A Story about Giighoonh and Tom Big Canoe, Sr.
(BARB MCDONALD, INTERVIEW, 2013)

In 1940, I was a little girl living on the Island with Gran and Grampa. One of our staple foods was fish. Now old Tom Big Canoe came by his name (*Giighoonh*—fishing) quite naturally, because there was nothing he liked to do better. He loved to fish. One day, I watched as he fashioned a soup spoon into a spinner for a large hook. Armed with lots of line and sinkers, he would go away out on our lake, when it was calm. He would be gone for quite a long time and there was always a good size trout for supper. Our fish then was tastier and fresh. This method of fishing was trolling—"*Daaigoke.*"

There was also a time in the fall to fish with nets (*Bigiidwaa*) and rods and line (*Mgiskan-an*). Grampa liked the first one, where we got a bunch of fish that had to be cleaned right away for the salt barrel. Reg and I helped a lot, and these had to be stored in a cold place. Mostly trout were salted. First he split open and gutted them, then piled them in the clean, wooden barrel. He layered the fish with coarse salt between each one.

These he gladly shared in the winter. Our fish dinners would be fish, boiled potatoes, warm scone, and tea—simple fare, but so delicious. That's the way it was. Good memories.

Ice Fishing

Lake Simcoe is well-known in southern Ontario for its ice fishing. As we have seen, this was first practiced by the Georgina Island people.

Jack Snake ice fishing

THE HUT SLEEPER SNEAKER
BY ROB PORTE

In the younger days, Mitts and I operated an ice fishing business. When the lake froze in the winter, we would take groups of two or four men out to the perch grounds and put them in one of our fifteen huts, provide minnows and pick them up just before dark.

Sounds easy, eh? You start every morning an hour before sunrise, earlier on Saturday and Sunday. I mean every morning. Winter here can last a long time but all huts must be on shore by March 15, therefore a small time period to make all your money. It can be done, but lots can go wrong. Fish huts have to be moved from time to time so we can stay over the fish. Our huts were back-breakers; it was all we could do to barely lift them. We would barely lift them. We would chip them free of the ice, pry them up enough to get a finger hold, both guys get a grip, "1, 2, 3, Lift!" Then we would lay the propane tank on its side, rest the weight of the hut on it [not recommended here] and try to catch our breath. Now more easily we could lift it the rest of the way up, back a heavy-duty sleigh under and pull off-load the hut, position it, block it up.

Then we would cut a new hole in the ice about 2 feet x 5 feet, off-load the hut, position it, block it up with some wood scraps to slow the rate at which the hut melts into the ice, and bank it with snow to keep the wind out. Sometimes we would tilt them all, then move them all, then cut them all, position, block and bank. This can take all day.

One day we saw a guy pulling a hand sleigh go inside one of our huts that was already tilted and ready to move. He didn't see us. We went about our business for about half an hour until it came time to move this next hut. We drove up into position and the sleigh was gone so we thought the guy was too. When we lifted the hut for loading, "1, 2, 3, Lift!" the fool was sleeping on a higher side bench with his sleigh inside. He rolled out, bounced once and flopped backward through the floorboard and into the lake. We helped him out, but he made it sound like it was our fault. We reminded him that he was breaking and entering (though the doors are never locked), there was no fish there anyway and (most thankfully) there were two of us and only one of him. He was so mad he wouldn't even take a ride to shore. Oh well, have a nice day. We've got work to do. (*The Georgina Island Storytelling Project*, 2006, p. 43)

CHAPTER EIGHT

Going to War

Georgina Island people have long responded to the call to fight for their territory. In the introduction, you read about how the people fought their way south into the Lake Simcoe area in the late 17th century. The story is told that as many as 500 canoe-loads of warriors, coming from as far away as Sault Ste. Marie, came into the Georgian Bay area in the 1690s. British and later Canadian governments could depend on the people to fight for their country. The following are stories that tell of how the people carried on this tradition.

The 18th and 19th Centuries

The Anishinaabe fought alongside the British in the American Revolution and together with other Canadians and the British against the same common American enemy in the War of 1812. In the latter war, they were part of an estimated 7,410 Anishinaabe warriors (a majority of the Indigenous contingent of over 10,000) that joined the British. It is reckoned that men from the bands of Georgina Island, Beausoleil Island/Christian Island, and Rama/Mjikaning contributed at least around 70 warriors/soldiers to the war effort, including being involved with the defense of York (Allen, 1992, p. 220).

Snake Islanders were part of a contingent that included the people from Rama and Beausoleil Island helping to present a show of government force in the Rebellions of 1837–8[31] by marching down Yonge Street during the hostilities. A message was sent that the rebels had to consider. This long march from their land triggered ill-conceived rumours among many York County farmers (including my Scottish ancestors who lived in the area) that a large scale "Indian raid" was taking place north of Toronto. This was a rumour started by settlers raised on stories passed down from New York and Pennsylvania family members of raids that took place during the American Revolution (Steckley, 2019, pp. 98–112).

---

31. For a description of the Rebellions of 1837–8, see Andrew McIntosh (2013), "The Rebellions of 1837–8," in *The Canadian Encyclopedia*.

After their long march, and their show of strength, the warriors were asked/demanded by Lieutenant Governor Francis Bond Head to stay for the winter in their temporary hunting camps at Holland Landing as an implied threat to the rebels, some of whom were based in that area. It was a cold winter, and the provisions promised by the Lieutenant Governor were very slow in coming. But the Anishinaabe warriors remained, keeping their part of the agreement despite the hardships they had to endure.

At the other end of the nineteenth century, at least one Georgina Islander, William Ashquabe (who would fight in World War I), may have been part of the Canadian contingent fighting alongside Britain in the Boer War (1889–1909) that was fought in South Africa.

The 20th and 21st Centuries

Georgina Islanders fought in all the major conflicts that involved the Canadian armed forces in the 20th century: World War I, World War II, the Korean War, the Gulf War, and the Afghanistan War. When most people think of Aboriginal fighters, they have a picture of Hollywood warriors. In the two world wars, Aboriginal people enlisted in high numbers. Take a good look at the faces presented in the pictures below. They are what brave faces of Aboriginal soldiers looked like in the 20th and the 21st centuries.

World War I

When you think of the 15 men from Georgina Island who fought in World War I, it is important to keep in mind that each one of them was a volunteer. Because of their having "Indian" status, they would not be forced or conscripted into fighting in the war, as were some other Canadians. It was their personal choice to risk their lives for their country. Some were still teenagers (e.g., Ross Peters, born in 1898), and some were in their 40s (e.g., Joseph Henry Ashquabe and William Ashquabe).

In the *Annual Report of the Department of Indian Affairs* for 1918, certain bands were selected for special mention of the high percentage of volunteers from their communities. Georgina Island was one of those bands. The reason for this special mention was that:

> ... these bands have sent to the front practically all their able-bodied male members of military age... These are records which cannot be surpassed by any community in the Dominion. (Scott, 1918, p. 25)

Herbert (Herb) Big Canoe volunteered for both world wars. He enlisted in 1915 when he was in his teens and 25 years later while in his early 40s. He served in World War I from 1915 to 1918. Like several other Georgina Island soldiers, he joined the 127th Battalion or York Rangers (as they recruited in York County). In 1916, they were renamed the 2nd Battalion, Canadian Railroad Troops, which became well-known for constructing light railway lines near the war front. In 1918, using guns they "liberated" from battle sites, they confronted the German army. In World War II, Herb was engaged from January 1940 to August 1945, meaning that in total he spent more than seven and a half years of serving his country. He survived both wars, although briefly, in the second war, he was reported as missing, to deep concern back home, followed by heartfelt relief when he was "found" again.

Georgina Islanders Involved in World War I

Bill Ashquabe	Enoch Big Canoe
Edward (Ed) Johnson	Robert Porte
Duncan Ashquabe	Herbert Big Canoe
James Johnson	George Vernon
Joseph Henry Ashquabe	Tom Big Canoe, Sr.
Ross Peters	Samson (Sam) York
Roger Ashquabe	John Bird

Alfred Porte

A Georgina Soldier Sends a Letter to His Grandfather

Somewhere in Belgium
Sept. 12, 1917

My Dear Grandfather,

In reply to your letter of July 8, which came to hand last night I am indeed very pleased to hear from you once more, as I have been expecting a letter from you all the time, and I am always pleased to get a letter from you. For you give me such good advice, which I know would do me a world of good if I should follow them.

The other letter last fall, well I kept that in my pocket and I would often read it until I could almost recite it, but I have handled it so much that it wore to pieces. But now since I have got this one I will have it in better keeping, as that is all the advice I get.

Our Regimental Chaplin left us quite a while ago and now is in some base hospital, although we have a chaplin which visits us about once a month, but it is always a short sermon that we hardly remember it. I am very sorry to say that I have received no Bibles from our Missionary Mr. W. E. Jones. I got a letter from Enoch Big Canoe quite a while ago letting me know that he got a letter from you and that there was some Bibles coming. But I believe they must have gone astray like this letter you sent me. For you sent your letter to the 2nd Canadian Troops. That is why I believe they have been lost, which I am very sorry for.

Your letter had to go to the Canadian Record Office at London, where every man is known. But I can't say if they send parcels there or not. However, I will make inquiries as I would be very pleased to have a Bible from Georgina Island and if they should come, I will distribute them among the boys from Georgina Island.

I am glad that we manage to keep together since we came to France. Those are sappers, Geo. Vernon, Duncan Ashquabe, Herb Big Canoe; there are four of us in this Unit and Ed Johnson is in England. I believe that he was invalided from France, and I believe that Ross Peters is in France too, in the 7th Canadian Railway Troops. It is too bad that we separated, but that can't be helped, and we are all in great hopes to get back home. And if the Almighty will spare us there will be great joy. But we are such a long ways from home just now. One would think that it is almost impossible to get home, but we came here so I guess we can get back.

We are having some very fine weather here the last couple of weeks, but I have been told that there is an early fall in this country. But I hope that it will not be so miserable as it was last winter. Well, Grandpa I guess this will be all for now, I am well. Hoping these few lines will find you and all of your family in the best of health. Thanking you again for your kind advice, I remain your Grandson.

                        778941 Corp'l J. S. York
                        D Company
                        2nd Canadian Railway Troops
                        c/o Arivy Post Office
                        London, England B. E. F.

P.S. I thank you very much for Photo you sent me, indeed you look well.

Note from Andy Big Canoe: This letter was written by Sam York (Donald

York and Fran Taylor's father) to my Great grandfather Charlies Big Canoe during the 1st World War.

(Editor's note: Some minor spelling and punctuation errors have been silently corrected for the sake of readability.)

The letter mentions "sappers," a term derived from the French word "sappe," referring to trenches. Sappers are soldiers who perform what can be called military engineering. This can involve digging trenches, building bridges, laying or clearing landmines, demolition, as well as road and airfield construction and repair. For a description of the Canadian Railway Troops, to which Corporal York was assigned, you may find of interest the Canadian Military Engineers Association article, "Canadian Railway Troops: A Brief History" (https://cmea-agmc.ca/canadian-railway-troops-brief-history).

It should be added that Sam York did arrive safely home in Georgina Island after his harrowing time as a sapper.

Top: Georgina Island War Veterans

Below:
Sam York and Enoch Big Canoe

A People of Stories

*Left:
Robert Porte
(2 photographs)*

*Far left:
George Vernon
Left:
Alfred Porte*

Below right, at bottom of page: Thomas Big Canoe

Left: Herb Big Canoe and Ed Johnson

Below left: Back row—George Vernon, Duncan Ashquabe, Herb Big Canoe, Ed Johnson and Ross Peters. Front row—Sam York and Nick Big Canoe

Two Thomas Big Canoes Go to War: Father and Son and Two World Wars
Thomas H. Big Canoe was born on January 17, 1886. By the time of the 1911 census, he had a wife, Hannah Port Big Canoe, and two children, Clifford, then three years old, and Olive Edna, then a one-year-old. He enlisted in the Canadian Expeditionary Force on March 24, 1917, at the age of 31, and gave his occupation as farmer. He had tried to enlist before, but was turned down because of "foot trouble" (which could have involved flat feet, hammer toes, or bunions). Anything that would make quick marching or walking a long way difficult was liable to disallow a potential soldier. His younger brother Enoch, born July 7, 1892, had tried to enlist almost two years earlier, on September 8, 1915, but was disqualified because of "flat feet." His second attempt at enlistment was successful a year later.

Thomas ended up in the Canadian Forestry Corps (CFC). The CFC made a significant contribution to the war effort by clearing 100 airfield sites and cutting some 814,000,000 board feet (a board foot measures 12 inches by 12 inches by 1 inch) of wood, making the British army self-sufficient in their many timber needs. As a Georgina Islander, Thomas Big Canoe, Sr., no doubt would have been highly skilled in cutting down trees and working with wood.

Thomas Beresford Big Canoe
Born after his father Thomas H. Big Canoe returned from what came to be called "the war to end all wars," Thomas Beresford Big Canoe (1926–1945) enlisted as a private in the Royal Hamilton Light Infantry in World War II, and was killed in action on March 8, 1945, in the Netherlands at the young age of 19. (The war in Europe ended only two months later.) He is buried in the Groesbeek Canada War Cemetery in the Netherlands, near the German border, and where 2,610 members of the British Commonwealth armed forces are buried, including many Canadians. Big Canoe is one of two Georgina Islanders to be laid to rest in a war cemetery in Europe.

As it says on his tombstone, "He died so that others may live."

Left: Donald York (1927–2010) and Thomas Big Canoe, Jr. (1926–1945)

A People of Stories

William (Bill) Ashquabe

William (Bill) Ashquabe not only survived World War I (and possibly the Boer War before that), but by 1951, when he was interviewed by Bill Riddell, a reporter for the *Newmarket Era*, in the feature "News of the Indians on Georgina Island," he was reported to be the oldest member of the Georgina Island band. His remembrances make for some interesting reading:

> The other day, we had a talk with Bill Ashquabe who is 77 years old and is the oldest inhabitant of Georgina Island. Except for being a little deaf, Mr. Ashquabe is just as good as he was 30 years ago. His only regret is that he hasn't been fishing in over 30 years. We asked him if he thought there would be an early spring. He replied that in the old days cold weather with a lot of snow was a forerunner of an early spring. He doesn't think it is as cold as it used to be. "In the old days, you could hear the trees cracking at night from the frost, but you don't hear that any more." We asked Mr. Ashquabe if he thought that the young Indians were as hardy as the old fellow. This brought an emphatic "No" from Mr. Ashquabe. "Don't see how they could be," he went on. "We old fellers used to get lots of wild meat, but these young ones don't know what it tastes like. They get too many fruits and vegetables. That's not good for them you know." "What about the language?" we asked. "When I was a boy, everyone knew the Indian tongue and some of us couldn't speak English. But now when I speak Indian to some of my young nephews and nieces, they just look at me… I guess they don't know what I'm talking about." We asked Mr. Ashquabe what he thought the world needed most. "More wild meat," he replied without batting an eye. (Riddell, 1951)

World War II Veterans

An estimated 44 different individuals from Georgina Island signed up to fight in World War II. All the men who were eligible to volunteer did so. In the words of Diane Trumble: "The men marched right up the road on this little island. Bagpipes were playing and my mother and all her siblings were crying and waving goodbye" (Sgambati, 2015).

James Ashquabe	Amos Charles
Joe Johnson	Harold Porte
Joe Snake*	Mary Ashquabe
Clayton Charles	Ron Johnson
Harry Porte	Merle Snake
Stephen Ashquabe	W. Harris Charles
Stanley Johnson	Jim Porte
Dave Trumble	Bill Big Canoe
Leonard Charles	Bert McCue
Mick Porte	Jim York
Percy Charles	Harold McCue
Tom Porte	Graydon Big Canoe
Ralph Charles	Harvey McCue
Angus Scelbe	Herb Big Canoe
Tom Charles	Morris McCue
Fred Sillaby	John Big Canoe
Edward Johnson	Stewart McCue
Harry Sillaby	Thomas Big Canoe
George Johnson	Walter McCue
John Snache, Jr.	Ken Blackbird
Herb Johnson	Garnet Porte

Jack Snake

*His name is given as "Joe Snache" in the picture below.

Left: Thomas Big Canoe, Jr.

Centre: Tom Porte; Amos and Leonard Charles. Right: Jim York, Sr.

A People of Stories

Above left: Stewart McCue.
Above centre: Joe Snache.
Above right: Stanley and Ida Johnson.

Above:
Lorna and Harris Charles.
Centre: Nicholas Big Canoe.
Right: Harold and Burt McCue.

Far left: Angus Scelbe, World War II veteran, band councillor 1963–7, 1973–7 and 1979–81, and Chief of Georgina Island from 1983 to 1989.
Left: Harris Charles and family.

"Indian Life Tops Germany: Cake 'N Coffee Greeting for Veterans"
In the November 16, 1948,[32] edition of *The Toronto Telegram*, an article appeared about two young men from Georgina Island, John Big Canoe and Fred Sillaby—his surname is given inaccurately as "Selby" in the article—who had just returned home after fighting in Europe in World War II for a year.

Two fighting men of the Otter totem—web belts loose and mouths full of apple pie—listened happily to the Ojibway chatter around them last night and decided it sounded better than anything they heard in Hannover.

John Big Canoe, 19, and Fred Selby, 24, home to their reservation [reserve] here after a year in Germany with the Algonquin Regiment of the 27th Brigade, figured it might be a long time before they did any more soldiering. The island looked too good.

Tribesmen, women and children from every house on the reservation jammed the community hall last night for a coffee and cake welcome and a chance to do a little singing.

Big Canoe and Selby ambled cheerfully from group to group dangling baby brothers and cousins and accepting the admiration of dozens of teenagers.

For several whites present the two men turned to English again—long enough to nail down published reports that life in the 27th was pretty unhappy.

"Overseas we heard all the talk about morale in the outfit being low, about the Germans avoiding us and how we complained about the British food," remarked Selby.

"Nobody told how German families took us into their homes for Christmas dinner. And we worked too hard to be low in morale. Why the longest time I ever spent in bar[r]acks was two weeks. We were out on manoeuvres nearly all the time."

"We began to get just a little tired of tents," smiled John Big Canoe

"Sure some of the guys made fools of themselves but they were only individuals," Fred Selby said, "Most of us were happy, well-trained troops. We figured we could hold off a Russian advance for a week, long enough for reinforcements to reach us."

---

32. I am not absolutely sure of the year that the article appeared.

The two Indians were pretty much at home in the Algonquin regiment, 45 per cent of which is Canadian Indian.

"We didn't seem to have many Indian officers though," recalled Big Canoe. "Most of the boys figured they were better off as privates."

Were they going to re-enlist? No, sir. They'd had enough of the army. Besides, there was fish to catch, money to make and a whole lot of singing to do. (Courtesy of the Georgina Island Storytelling Project)

John Big Canoe, 19, (left) and Fred Selby, 24, happily flank their grandmothers at homecoming party. Left is Mrs. Harriet Charles, Big Canoe's grandmother, right is Mrs. Arthur Selby.

Mary Ashquabe

You may have noticed one female name in the list of Georgina Island soldiers in World War II. What made a young woman from Georgina Island, a teenager born in 1923, enlist in the Canadian armed forces during World War II? That was what Mary Ashquabe did on her 19th birthday, February 23, 1942. She ended up in the Royal Canadian Air Force Women's Division,[33] and served her country until February 16, 1943. She was among the first of 72 Indigenous women who enlisted in the Canadian Armed Forces in World War II. None served in World War I, as they were not given permission.

The "WDs," as they were known, were newly named the month that Mary enlisted, and had an active recruitment drive for women (the first of the Canadian armed forces to do so), with posters that declared "She serves that

---

33. For information about the Women's Division, see March and de Bruin, 2016 and 2023.

Top: Mary Ashquabe.
Below:
Mary and Myra Snake.

men might fly… Enlist today in the RCAF." She leaped at the opportunity as soon as it appeared. By the end of the war, 17,038 women had served in the Women's Division, and 30 had died in active service.

She rose in the ranks from Aircraftwoman Second Class to First Class, leaving the armed forces as Leading Aircraftwoman. Her work with the RCAF was listed as "General Duties" and "Cook". Her Commanding Officer, D. Edwards, Group Captain, filled in her Attestation Form, saying that "His conduct and character" was "Very Good," and that "His qualifications" were "Satisfactory." The forms apparently did not acknowledge the gender of women in the Air Force.

Merle Snake

Merle George Snake was born on September 1, 1907. He enlisted in the 5th Field Company of the Royal Canadian Engineers, a company that went overseas early in 1942. As a sapper, his often dangerous duties would have included being one of the first to land on beaches to take care of the demolition of land mines and other unexploded bombs and hazardous materials, and building and repairing roads and bridges. His company was involved with the Allied landings in Normandy during the spring and summer of 1944. He died in battle on July 6, 1944, at age 36, and is buried in Beny-Sur-Mer Canadian War Cemetery, in Calvados, Normandy. On his gravestone his mother, Mary L. Snake, had engraved the words: "In Memory of Merle, home at last, the labour done, the battle, the victory won, Mother."

Tom Porte

In a ceremony honouring Canada's First Nations war veterans held on November 8, 2015 (November 8 being, since 1997, Aboriginal Veterans Day), Dianne Trumble brought her grandfather Tom Porte's battered helmet from World War II. She was quoted as saying, "I'm just so proud of him. It's got a lot of dents in it. I imagine it's been through a lot" (Sgambati, 2015).

By then, none of Georgina Island's Second World War veterans remained alive. When she was interviewed by a reporter, Dianne Trumble spoke of her grandfather's remembrance of the war: "He never talked about it. It was something he never spoke of. He often talked about not being treated the same as the other veterans because he was native" (Sgambati 2015).

Honouring Tom

There were many ways in which Aboriginal veterans were treated as second class. They received significantly less in post-war financial benefits, including disability pensions, war service gratuities, dependents' allowances, re-establishment grants, and education and training provisions. Their role in the war was not until relatively recently recognized in books, and in a hugely negative symbolic way, until 1992 they had not been permitted to place a wreath on the national cenotaph at the same ceremony with other veterans on November 11.

Harold McCue

Other Veterans

Two of the World War II veterans fought also in the Korean War (1950–53): Graydon Big Canoe and Harry Sillaby. Kevin Big Canoe is a veteran of the Gulf War (1990–91), and J. Big Canoe of the Afghanistan War, which Canada participated in from 2001 to 2014.

CHAPTER NINE

The Crossing: The Challenge of Living on an Island

When the people moved to Snake Island and then to Georgina Island, Lake Simcoe was significantly shallower than it is today. Crossing between the mainland and the islands was much simpler and safer. At certain spots well known to the community, people could wade across, ride on horseback, or take a wagon drawn by horses, following a traditional footpath across from the islands to the mainland and back. It was a lot like fording a river where you know where the best place is to cross. On Georgina Island they could use the Sand Islands off the southeast of the island like stepping stones the first part of the way. This was the way of things for the people for over a century.

Another much-valued benefit of the shallow waters between island and mainland during those years was that there were paddies of *menomin*

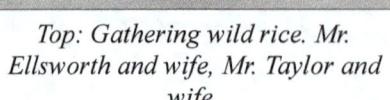

Top: Gathering wild rice. Mr. Ellsworth and wife, Mr. Taylor and wife.
Below: Rice harvesting beater. Canadian Museum of History, III-G-371, 3191-211-0079-D2003-06748

('good grain') or wild rice that people could harvest with wooden wild rice beaters, which were something like paddles. These were expertly carved by skilled Georgina Island men such as Orrice Coates' grandfather, who carved the rice beater illustrated here. Of course they would also have carved paddles for their canoes in a similar manner. Many of those were sold to the growing settler population.

There were also cranberry marshes along the shores of Georgina Island, where more good food could be harvested each year at about the same time as the rice.

This changed with the construction of the Trent-Severn Waterway. It runs some 386 kilometres, from the Lake Ontario port town of Trenton up the Trent River to Rice Lake, then up the Otonabee River, through the Kawartha lakes, flowing through canals that connected this system to Lake Simcoe and Lake Couchiching, and to the Severn River, which flows into Georgian Bay, part of Lake Huron. Its initial purpose was for the system to provide a passageway for commercial shipping, something it never became. The Trent-Severn Waterway was completed in 1920. And the water level of Lake Simcoe rose some three metres in the process, and the distance between Georgina Island and the mainland roughly doubled. According to Elder Andrew Big Canoe, on a clear day looking west you could see the old shoreline—maybe 200 to 300 yards out from the current one. The crossing between Georgina Island and the mainland became much more difficult and dangerous. And the wild rice and cranberry areas were drowned. It was only relatively recently (in 2014) that paddies of wild rice have been planted on the shores of the island to begin growing again a much loved and needed crop (see https://georginaisland.com/wp-content/uploads/2014/08/Wil-Wegman-Wild-Rice.pdf).

Stories of the Crossing

A good part of the cultural narrative of the Chippewas of Georgina Island involves stories of the crossing between island and mainland. Here are a few such stories. There are many more that have not been put into writing. They speak of the determination of the people to overcome difficult obstacles.

Winter Stories of the Past

During the winter there were many crossings, horse-drawn vehicles taking many trips for a variety of reasons: visiting friends and family, shopping, playing in and attending hockey games, hauling logs for people living on the mainland. And people had ice houses in which they would cut ice as a source of water in the winter.

Winter has its own challenges in terms of crossing, the lives of humans and horses being put at risk, but it also had some delights in years gone by. This story talks about the positive side of winter crossing.

Archie Blackbird and Reg Canoe

Skating Across the Ice to Watch the Sutton Greenshirts

Elder Albert Big Canoe tells the story of one of the most exciting forms of entertainment when he was growing up on Georgina Island. He and his friends would skate across the ice between island and mainland to Sutton to watch the Sutton Greenshirts play hockey against teams from other small towns in the area. Georgina Islanders added to the strength of the team. Henry, Mick, and Tom Porte were Greenshirts. A number of Big Canoes played for the team over the years: Buzz, Rudy, and Ted.

Buzz was a star defenceman for the Greenshirts in the late 1950s. He was generally a major force for hockey in the area, coaching, sponsoring teams and individuals that could not otherwise afford to play. It is fitting that in the town of Georgina there is now an annual fund-raising hockey tournament named after him. His contribution to local hockey continues even after his death in 2007 at 68 (see "Buzzy Big Canoe raises $2k," *Georgina Advocate*, March 7, 2013).

Sandra and Buzzy

In a letter to the editor in the *Newmarket Era* on July 17, 2007, headlined "Buzzy Big Canoe will always be remembered," a person whose family cottage was on Georgina Island wrote the following:

> Buzzy was always on call by my father-in-law George Kingwood to assist us in our many predicaments that we would find ourselves in on the island. I distinctly remember Buzzy and Clayton Charles rescuing us from the lake one Sunday in February after we got stuck in our return home. The water and slush was well over our boots and our three young daughters were greatly concerned. Buzzy and Clayton appeared and pushed our car out of the mess and slowly and quietly drove us to the mainland.

Buzzy was also chief from 1971 to 1981, and was heavily involved with efforts to improve the energy efficiency of people's homes. His daughter Donna became the first female chief of Georgina Island.

To learn more about his contributions to his people, see "Big Canoe remembered for leadership, volunteer spirit" in the *Newmarket Era* of July 10, 2007.

Reg, Buzz, and Barbara Big Canoe

*Top: Donna and Hugh (Buzzy) Big Canoe
Below: Donna Big Canoe, first elected as chief in 2007, and still chief in 2025*

Albert Big Canoe reckoned that the trip to Jackson's Point was about four miles (roughly 6.5 kilometres) each way. Still, on a moonlit night, the game was not the only entertainment on ice. Gliding across the lake with the ice reflecting the moon's light, the journey from the island to the mainland and back again was also part of the thrill. The potential danger of the journey on skates could add to the excitement for the young travellers.

But there could be real danger and potential loss of life in such a trip to watch a hockey game, as Elder Susan Hoeg reveals in the following story from around the same time:

A Miracle

One winter night in February of 1953, our local hockey team was playing a game at the Sutton Arena. My grandfather, George Vernon, and I walked across the frozen lake. We got a ride on the other side into town and we excitedly watched the game.

A raging snowstorm had started and when I saw some players and fans climbing into a car I begged my grandfather to let me join them, instead of making the long walk across the lake. I was ten years old. My grandfather firmly said, "No!" so we began the long cold walk home. The storm soon let up and soon the moon and stars were making our journey much easier. When we reached the shore someone told us the car hadn't made it over. Something was terribly wrong.

The car had no top. It had been cut off making it like a jeep. Ten people had climbed into the car, which belonged to Carl Lance of Virginia. His passengers were Dave and Joyce Trumble, Viola York, Lillian Big Canoe who was pregnant with Darlene, and there were Dick Charles, Marjorie (Marge) Blackbird, Bill Warren, Delores Ashquabe and her younger sister Clara. In the raging storm they got off the main ice road and were near Duclos Point when they hit a pressure crack. The car went down and most [of it] ended up in the icy water. Carl, who still had on his hockey equipment, pulled one by one out of the freezing water. Lillian floated on a piece of ice. Marge was in the lake and as she was about to climb out someone would grab onto her pulling her back into the icy lake, icicles hung from her hair.

Miraculously everyone got out. Just about the time the storm passed, Delores remembers it being so bright with the moon and stars shining. As they walked she remembers the sound of cracking ice on Clara and Dick. Clara wanted to lie down and sleep but Delores shook her to keep her awake and to keep walking.

They were taken into the home of Don Shepherd and Alec Loc, where they were given shelter and food. Doctor Noble attended them. The next day the *Telegram*, a Toronto newspaper, reported the story. The title read "Nothing short of a miracle." The reporters used the home of Bud Joblin, where they sent pictures by wire to Toronto. They reported it was the first time photos were sent this way from this area.

When Delores and Clara arrived home, their Dad yelled and yelled until he couldn't yell anymore. Then sitting down he started to cry, he was so relieved to see them home. Our whole Island community was happy to have them all come home.

Albert Big Canoe: Horse and Buggy Crossing the Ice

There were a number of different ways of travelling across the ice in the old days. Albert Big Canoe speaks about one of them: "We'd take a horse and buggy. Tie her up at the shore. Cause she'd already eaten. And then we'd come back. She knew the way home. We'd jump in the buggy and cover up and then let her go. And she'd stop at the park" (Albert Big Canoe, n.d.).

More praise and respect for the Georgina Island horses can be found in the words of Elder Leonard Porte, who also mentions Lorenzo Big Canoe and his truck:

We had no cars or trucks here. We used work horses to travel, and walking. The horses would go over the ice road to travel to the general store on Hadden Road, which was Allen O'Neil's store. We would travel in very bad weather, snow and stormy, but those horses could go through anything. The horses knew their way home to the island. Later

Lorenzo Big Canoe had a truck. He would take community members to town on the ice and in the summer he ran a ferry. Lorenzo was the Chief and he was once a school teacher. He was a smart man. (Interview, October 25, 2014)

Treacherous Crossing

Crossing could be treacherous, as World War II army veteran and Snake Island caretaker Harold McCue found when he had to travel between Snake Island and the mainland to obtain much needed supplies to feed his family in 1949:

FAMILY STARVING—INDIAN RISKS SIMCOE ICE FOR FOOD

Fighting his way tortuously through piles of broken ice, Harold McCue, 35, Indian father of two small children, finally reached Snake Island a mile and a quarter out in Lake Simcoe with food and milk for his starving family and three other residents of the island, late Sunday.

Cut off from the main shore when the ice broke up making a crossing impossible, the island's seven Indian residents had been without decent food since Wednesday. Saturday, with the cries of his two children, aged 18 months and three, ringing in his ears, McCue desperately set out in a battered boat to get supplies. Pushing through a narrow opening in the ice he reached the main shore, bought his supplies at Bell's Groceteria and attempted to return. He found his path once again blocked with ice. Unable to return, the distraught Indian spent the night with a friend, Howard Charles.

From early Sunday morning on, Mrs. McCue could be seen frantically signally with a mirror. Late in the afternoon he borrowed a steel-bottomed boat from Bert Day, William Bell loaning him an outboard motor. Once again he set out to break through the ice-bound channel with desperately needed food. A crowd of spectators watched as time after time he was brought to a halt by the jammed ice. Finally after an hour and a half he broke through and reached the island. "This will never happen again," McKue told the crowd as he stepped onto the boat for the final attempt to reach his wife and kiddies. "My family will go to the city while the ice breaks up next spring," he said.

Snake Island is the property of the Chippewa Indians, whose main reservation is on 15-mile distant Georgina Island. McCue, a war veteran of six years overseas service, was appointed as caretaker of Snake Island last August by the Department of Indian Affairs. Living on the island besides

McCue and his family is Jim Ashquabe and his two sons, Duncan, 52, and Stanley, 45. (*Newmarket Era and Express*, April 14, 1949, p. 1)

Making the Crossing During the 1950s
ANDREW BIG CANOE (1938–2023; INTERVIEW)

When asked by an interviewer what he felt were major changes concerning life on Georgina Island over the last few decades, Elder Andrew Big Canoe answered with the following:

Andrew Big Canoe

That's one of the biggest changes, travel. Row boats and small motor boats probably in the middle early fifties, few around, fewer guys got them, and my father had no boat cover ... had a St Lawrence engine ... that one cylinder engine. He used to run people back and forth, he could carry about four people and himself ... probably in the early sixties, late fifties ... he bought a boat I think about twenty two feet long that would carry about eight or ten people and he used to run ferry here ... that was another big change ... ice, travelling on the ice ... as soon as the ice got two to three inches thick everybody walked over, all winter ... very few people had cars, maybe one or two or three cars over here and if they did, if it was drivable out, there was no one to plough the roads ... so if you had a snowstorm you couldn't go anywhere with a car ... but from the ferry landing, there was a landing. Where there was a small dock, they landed, probably where the marina is now. There was a big willow tree, a huge one. That's where everybody landed. And if you came there, and people went over and went over from coming over, from walking back and forth it was like a sidewalk, all the way to the island, there was a hollow sleigh, which is called a hand sleigh. You could put your groceries on or your elders that couldn't walk. You took your hand sleigh and stuck it in the snow bank over there and when you came back it was still there.

Lost on the Lake

As we saw earlier, students from Georgina Island who had graduated from the primary school on the island would often have to board on the mainland during the school months. They would still occasionally travel across to their island home to be with family and friends. Elder Susan Hoeg tells this story:

> On our way back to our boarding homes on the mainland, our car got stuck in a snow drift. I was on the lake with two younger cousins, Sandra and Charlotte. The three of us tried pushing, but it was no use.
>
> We decided to walk to shore, but with the blowing snow were soon lost. I got very sleepy and then I suddenly remembered that's how people freeze to death. I was just so tired; I wanted to sleep for a while before continuing on.
>
> Luckily, my two cousins didn't feel as I did. They took me by my arms, and we continued to walk against the driving snow. We eventually found the shoreline and following it came to our road.
>
> After walking another mile up this road, we stopped at my Auntie's home where we were given hot chocolate and a warm place by the woodstove to get warm. (Susan Hoeg, *The Georgina Island Storytelling Project*, 2006, p. 16)

Before telling the next story, we should inform you that the Indian Act prohibited the sale of alcohol to Indigenous people from 1884 to 1985, a little over a century (see Anonymous, "A Look at First Nations Prohibition of Alcohol," 2016). Legalized prejudice enabled this to happen.

The Tragedy of the Mounties

On June 7, 1958, five young RCMP officers (a 33-year-old sergeant, a 21-year-old constable and three 19-year-old constables) were travelling to Georgina Island because they knew that a wedding was being held there. Their superior officers felt that there was a good chance that alcohol would be drunk there, and their job was to stop it. At the time it was illegal for the Chippewas of Georgina Island to have or drink alcohol on the island, as it was for status Indians across Canada. That law would not change for almost 30 years.

While the officers were on their way crossing to the island, a fierce storm picked up and the kind of huge waves that can occur on the lake quickly rose up higher and higher. Eventually these dangerous waves would swamp the 14-foot motorboat that the five officers were travelling in. All were drowned. This would prove to be the largest single death toll in the then more-than-century-long history of the RCMP. Following the incident, and a long inquest, regulations concerning boat size and passenger number were changed to try to prevent further such tragedies. But ending the practice of arresting Indigenous people for purchasing alcohol would take another quarter of a century.

In 1978, the Georgina Island Police Service replaced the RCMP, with three police officers serving Georgina, Snake, and Fox Island, as well as responding to emergencies on Lake Simcoe. It is part of the larger First Nations Police Service.

Crossing in the 1960s

What happens when you give birth on the mainland, and you want to bring your newborn home to the island? And what if it is during that time that separates the dregs of winter from true spring, a time when no one mode of crossing can be considered to be completely safe? This story from Sandra Big Canoe gives an example of the danger that could result in the 1960s in those circumstances.

THE JOURNEY HOME

On April 9th, 1969, I delivered my second son at York County Hospital in Newmarket. My stay in the hospital was seven days and by the end of the week I was anxious to get back to my home on Georgina Island. Spring was here and the ice on the lake was getting quite soft. People were still crossing the frozen lake on foot. When my husband, Buzzy, arrived to take us home, he informed me that the baby and I would be crossing in a hand-pulled sleigh!

Our car pulled into Sibbald Point Park, where the last safe landing was being used by island residents to cross the lake. It was a warm sunny day, and as I held my precious bundle in my arms, I was pretty scared. I said a little prayer and was ready to make the journey home. Buzzy, my dad and Ron Charles took turns pulling me and my papoose on a toboggan over the very soft ice. The water kept coming up between the cracks at every step. They had a stick that they would push into the ice to make sure it was thick enough. Sometimes that stick went right through the ice. As we got closer to the island, we could see that the ice had moved away from the shore! Now we had to figure out a way to get on to dry land.

My mom, my five-year-old son Lenny, my sister Mary and Angus and Archie were on shore waiting for us. What were we going to do? As I watched, Angus and Archie laid wooden planks from the shore across the water to where we were stranded on the ice. The men were soaking wet from trudging through the icy water. They passed my little one from one to the other until he was on dry land. Then we all carefully crossed the makeshift bridge to safety.

Many times in those days, people traveled to and from the island when the lake was unsafe. Those of us who remember what it was like are very thankful to have safe, dependable traveling on our ferryboat and in the winter on the "scoot." I will never forget how scared I was the day my son Derek and I made the journey home through slush and ice. Or how grateful I was to the friends and family that helped to bring us home safely. (Sandra Big Canoe, *The Georgina Island Storytelling Project*, 2006, p. 27)

Crossing in the 1980s

Most of the stories of the crossing so far talk about the dangers of winter crossing. But summer can create its troubles as well, as we saw with the drowning of the Mounties. Sandra Big Canoe relates this story:

It was a warm summer day on May 30th, 1985. My eight-year-old daughter, Donna [later to become chief of her people], and I were coming home from a shopping trip. The wind had picked up and we were on the mainland, getting ready to catch the little ferry service to Georgina Island. The school children that attended school in town were catching the ferry too. There were about twenty-five people crowded on the ferry with their groceries. There were babies, school children, seniors and adults. We even had a mattress being held steady by some of the men on the back of the boat!

The driver, Eric Charles, was going to let his fourteen-year-old daughter, Lisa, drive the boat, but changed his mind when he saw that the wind was picking up. We were all anxious to leave the dock, as the wind was getting stronger. There was a storm coming from the direction of Barrie. We had already started out when the rain began. Thunder started to rumble in the sky. Eric thought we could beat the storm, but we got caught right smack in the middle of it. It was blowing so hard that Eric could not steer the ferryboat. Everyone was scared. I was fearful for my daughter, who was so little. I put a life preserver on her. There were only five or six on the boat at the time. I remember a little baby on the boat, and I was fearful for her life. The rain was so heavy, we could not see two feet in front of us.

The boat was rolling from side to side and I thought we would tip over and drown. I started to pray for our safety. Eric yelled at someone to throw out the anchor, but it would not hold. It seemed like an hour, but it was actually only a few minutes before the terrible storm passed. We were all scared and soaking wet, but grateful to have survived. Most of the community was waiting for us on shore as we neared the island dock. My husband, Buzzy, was upset that I was on the boat and told me I should have waited until the storm was over. Every family on the island had a member on the boat that day. What a near tragedy! Later on, we discovered that a tornado had hit the town of Barrie, and had passed right by us on Lake Simcoe. Sometimes it takes a close call like this to make you realize how precious our home and community is to us. (Sandra Big Canoe, *The Georgina Island Storytelling Project*, 2006, p. 11)

The Ferries

There have been various kinds and sizes of ferries crossing between Georgina Island and the mainland over the years. These include *Keche Chemon* ('big canoe'), *Chippewa Bezhig* ('one' or 'the first'), *Chippewa Ninzh* ('two' or 'the second'), and now *Aazhaawe*. The name given to the last-named vessel by Elder and longtime Anishinaabemowin language teacher Barb McDonald is derived from a verb meaning 'to cross,' the same verb from which the southern Ontario city name Oshawa traces its origin. The reason for choosing the name is told in the following passage from the Chippewas of Georgina Island First Nation website: "It is a phrase that has been commonly used by residents for many, many years. 'Are you going across?' or 'I'm going across today,' or 'Are you going across again?' are phrases that are part of life on the island."

Chippewa Bezhig

The ferry *Chippewa Bezhig* ran during the 1980s. Some of the difficulties of running this ferry are set out in the following story by Rob Porte, entitled "My New Job":

Back in the days of *Chippewa One*, the old barge, we faced a lot more risk and adventure. The *Chippewa Bezhig* you see down Simcoe was 6 feet narrower and 18 feet shorter, the wheelhouse was on the deck and we cranked the landing platform by hand. The improvements made in the winter of '88 helped big time. Before then, we had to bring smaller loads of everything, no cement trucks. Concrete blocks and septic tanks had to be deck loaded and manually removed on the Island. The largest truck we could take was a single axle dump. We would land at the end of the steel dock, chain to shore as close as we could to the wall; you had to get the tip of the ship's deck on top of the steel dock before you lowered the ramp. We had to clamp the chain tighteners "bear traps," and work the boat back and forth to get every bit you could. Lower the ramp carefully because if your hand slipped off the crank, she could spin back and split your skull.

Now the fun part, there were two 16-foot hardwood planks 18 inches wide and 4 inches thick, weighing over 200 pounds each. Chain loops at each end were used as handles to move them. Two men would drag the plank half on shore and line up with the truck tires and back it on. Very, very slowly centred it, left and right, once the rear tire got on the plank we had to readjust the end. If the truck driver turned his steering wheel after that, we would have to start all over, or worse. As the truck came back the weight was transferred onto the ship's deck, nice and slow and you had to find a good place to stand. One guy on each side of the truck watching the plank, the barge's buoyancy, the chains and the loading ramp; you had to be on the deck, away from the chains in case they snapped, and be able to see the other crewman and the truck driver because the barge motors were full ahead to help hold the wall. If the front tires line up, beautiful! Back her up all the way until the planks are free, pull them onto the deck out of the way and bring the truck back forward almost to the centre of buoyancy.

As the truck was adjusting, the loading ramp would be flapping up and down like a fish on the floor. The ramp was made of steel about

12 feet by 8 feet, and must have weighed 1,000 pounds. I hoped no onlookers would get too close. As the truck adjusted, the chain may slacken and we would get the bear traps off and one chain. Crank the ramp up, remove the last chain, as the boats drifted over, climb back on and get away from the ramp. As we disembarked, the barge would slide off the dock and the gate would catch and slam all the way to the top, I mean WHAM! The barge would bob a bit, a little unsettling to first timers, and then we backed away towards the wind. Driving lesson tomorrow. Earned a break, half-hour to the island, smoke 'em if you got 'em. Landing on the island was very difficult in the wind. We landed on the end back then. The chain up moment was in relation to the wind, drift, buoyancy, dock, ramp and plank length. You'll catch on. The planks would want to kick out because the truck tires push, but once started it usually came off nice. But stay away from those chains, the ramp and planks could kick out at any moment, so pay attention!

I threw my right hand at the rail but the Skidoo suit was too bulky for me to reach it.

There were lots of challenges that first shipping season and into early winter. We could just squeeze four cars on and had to move the planks onto the dock near Christmas time. So the deck had more room for walk-on passengers. Those planks were heavy and when I lifted my end. Half the loop broke and I slipped at the edge of the loop in the other hand and plank was sliding away from shore and wanting to pile drive into lake. My right hindquarter was in the water completely. My left foot caught high. I let go of the loop and Rob Big Canoe, my fellow crewman, pulled the plank back. My left hand was slipping. I threw my right hand at the rail but the skidoo suit was too bulky for me to reach it. Thank heaven old Link Taylor was right there, caught my hand and pulled me just in time. A split second later I was fully in 12 feet of ice-cold water with a skidoo suit, rubber boots and a four-foot climb out with 50 people watching.

Meegwetch boys! Link was pushing 60 years old and I was over 200 pounds with all my gear on, but he plucked me off the edge like I was a little kid. Anyway, I think I like this kind of work; hopefully they'll keep me on. (Rob Porte, *The Georgina Island Storytelling Project*, 2006, p. 19–20)

The Scoot

The scoot is a winter lifesaver for the people of Georgina Island. It is a 5.4-metre flat-bottomed air boat, with three large blades powered by a 350-horsepower engine. Since the mid-1980s it has been part of the daily winter life of Georgina Island schoolchildren who have graduated from the island school, *Wabigoon-gamig* ('Blossoming House'), which runs to grade five, and then have to further their education on the mainland. The scoot enables them to go to school on the mainland, and return, without having to board with people there. It also provides the adventure for the day. There are three of them currently operating. Rob Porte, of the previous story, has long been one of the drivers.

If you want to know what riding a scoot is like, a few words can help you: loud (the driver wears headphones, and not for music), bumpy (particularly if the temperature has been rising and falling, with melting and freezing), a little scary sometimes, but still fun.

Top: Rob Porte and Derek Big Canoe honoured for community service.
Second from top: Porte family.
Middle: The Scoot.
Bottom: Lorenzo Big Canoe driving the ferry.

A People of Stories

Top row, left: Clarence Porte and his son Larry Porte.
Top row, right: Chippewa Niizh.
Second row, left: First ferry.
Second row, centre: Munroe McCue.
Second row, right: Norm Charles.
Bottom row, left: Water taxi.
Bottom row, right: John Big Canoe in boat.

Chapter Ten

Growing Up on Georgina Island in the Not-Too-Distant Past

The following stories told by Barbara McDonald (née Big Canoe) about growing up on Georgina Island are taken from *Ngoding* ('At One Time'), *The Georgina Island Storytelling Project*:

> On a beautiful spring morning birds singing awaken me, robins chirping and blackbirds clucking and clicking. It is hard not to reflect back to my childhood, to the many things our maternal grandfather had taught us. Every spring, *Mnookmi*, is a fresh start he would say. My cousin and I would go into the bush for some of these new wild and wonderful things. The burgundy and white trilliums and there was also a flower we called Jack-in-the-Pulpit, the Dutchman's Britches, tiny blue, yellow and white violets and of course, the real purpose of our trek in the bush, morels. These delicious mushrooms are difficult to find but with effort we would fill up our peach baskets and journey home.
>
> Our Gran would tell us to clean them, cut them in half and wash them thoroughly, then soak them in salt water overnight. Yes, we would sometimes have them for breakfast with warm scone washed down with hot sugared tea, simple but so nourishing. Lunch would be fresh perch, potatoes and bread and then back to school we would go. When school was out at four, we came home to do chores. Mine was to fill the reservoir on the stove with water so we would have warm water to wash the supper dishes. The boys would chop wood, pile some and then carry it in. Supper might be salt pork or pork jowl, fried, potatoes or beans and of course, more scone and tea. The dishes would be washed and put away so the table would be available for games like Parcheesi or cribbage. We played by lamplight, good old coal oil. Our evenings were not late, everyone would be tucked in bed by 10:30 p.m. or 11:00 p.m., no later, and we had to be careful of our lamp oil.

Our way of life was beautiful and natural. My cousin and I would play outside by the field beside our old house. There was an apple tree we used to climb and you know sometimes apple trees can be prickly and awkward, anyway, my cousin picked what he wanted, put them in his pocket and slid down and there I was in the tree! I picked my apple and of course had no pocket. I was so scared holding on with only one hand. I promptly fell from the tree. I was hurt, but not seriously, cut mouth and bruised ankle. My poor cousin carried me running across the field as fast as he could so Gran could fix me up. I was only about seven years old, and my cousin was nine. I was fine in a couple of days.

On another one of our adventures in the woods, around Christmas, we always got to find and chop down our own tree. This particular time we left after school and went straight back from Grandpa's place. Now the snow was fairly deep in some places, which made it difficult for me being small and short, but I kept up. It seems we walked and walked and still he had not spotted a tree to his liking. It was getting dark and I knew my cousin got turned around. He said we must get back. Now I was really scared. We kept on walking then we sat for a bit so he could listen. He was determined to get us home before it got pitch dark. As we were walking he suddenly stopped, holding me by the arm now, he said, "Don't be scared, I hear the bells, we will just keep walking towards the sound." What had happened was our grandparents were aware we were very late and it was dark and unlike us to stay in the woods that long. They got the idea to ring the church bell so we could hear it. We were both so very tired by now but we kept trudging on. Soon we saw an opening and a road, and then we could hear Grandpa's team of horses. We were so happy. He and my Uncle had hay and blankets on the sleigh and my cousin and I thought, "Boy, we are really going to get heck!" but we didn't. We were reminded not to venture into the bush late in the day. But we did get our Christmas tree, the next day. Early!

"The calf made a swift turn, hit a nearby tree and we all tumbled out."
In the winter we would go sliding down at the lake, and skate when the lake froze over. Grandpa had some cows and horses and this one time my cousin made a harness for the calf and he hitched him onto a sleigh. Well, we got on the old flat sleigh and there were three of us,

Barbara Big Canoe

and it was too heavy for the little calf and he started running real fast and bucking and kicking. We all hung on for dear life. We were laughing and yelling and just as were told what would happen, it did. The calf made a swift turn, hit a nearby tree and we all tumbled out. Thank goodness no one was hurt, the sleigh was broken up and we had a hard time catching that little calf though!

The winter was a great time, the teams of horses would travel with cords of wood and people would hitch a ride over to get groceries, usually on a Saturday. It was also hockey time in Sutton. Our own men and boys would play against the Sutton Green Shirts. This would cause an exodus from the Island. Some walked over, others who were lucky enough got to ride with a team. The games were always so exciting, fast, sometimes rough, but a good time was had by all.

Then of course, maple sugar time was not far behind. This was also an enjoyable time. They would take a team of horses to the bush, laden with all the utensils, boiling kettles, spiles, pails to catch the sweet sap, and you also took your lunch and goodies to cook in the open fire. You would be gone for a whole day, the end result being jars of beautiful syrup and candy and a wonderful experience.

These memories are as vivid as if they happened yesterday. Our times of growing up in the early '40's on the Island were good. We were never hungry, certainly never bored, we made our own happenings. My cousin Reg was a person who could snare rabbits, hunt ducks and fish, was good a woodsman and a beautiful singer. I have written these short stories to honour his memory. He passed away July 20th, 2003.

Our home was a nice log house, a little farm, horses, cows and chickens on Georgina Island with Tom and Hannah Big Canoe, Cliff (Chowie) and Hugh and us two.

"*Mii-go-geget,*" that's for sure.

The Island Fire

In 1955, there was a big fire on Georgina Island. It was especially dangerous as there was no indoor plumbing at the time, no fire hydrants to attach hoses to, and no way a fire truck could make it to the island. Here is a story of that fire from Elder Susan Hoeg:

> The fire burned at a terrifying speed. With no fire-fighting equipment, our island was in terrible danger of being completely burned.
>
> The summer of 1955 was hot and dry, thirty-eight days of no rain made the bush land very dry. That night as I lay in bed, my grandmother, Delina, gently told me that we might have to leave our home in a hurry if the fire got too close. I stared up at the ceiling, watching shadows from the burning oil lamp. We talked about what we would take. It wouldn't be much because we [would] have to leave in a small rowboat that my grandfather, George, had built. We were only a few minutes from the boathouse where our boat would take us to safety.
>
> The fire burned on the north east side. Cattle grazed near the area. Our people worked day and night, carrying pails of water and fighting the fire with shovels and axes. Volunteer workers, firemen from local fire departments, OPP and RCMP officers answered our emergency calls for help. Mainland community and church organizations, merchants and the Salvation Army donated food. The women made hampers of food and drinks, tramping through the bush to take food to the tired workers. My mother Mary [the WWII veteran] remembers dragging a large hose through the bush with her friend Mona. The 1½-mile hose was rushed to the island by the Mount Albert Fire Department.
>
> Later, [with] a shift in the wind, and all the work done by the volunteers, the fire was finally under control, answering the prayers of our people. (*The Georgina Island Storytelling Project*, 2006, p. 15)

The 100-Year-Old Church

One part of growing up on Georgina Island from the time of first settlement there until 1964 was the old Methodist church. It was erected in 1864, as Charles Big Canoe noted in his narrative, and the effort to do so was monumental. The story goes that it had been a church in Bradford, was taken apart there, and was moved to Georgina Island by a team of horses that eventually took the major pieces of the church across the ice to the island. In 1964, after standing for a century, it was replaced by the current United Church.

Left: First church in the 1800s. Right: The church today.

The Trumbles

Freda Trumble tells this story:

When I was born [in] December of 1956, life was pretty tough back then.

We did not have hydro or running water. All we had was oil lanterns, outhouses and wood stoves. When we needed water, my brother and sisters would go down to the lake and bring water home for bathing, cooking and cleaning. Sometimes we would spill it, and then we'd have to go all the way back down to the lake to get more. It got to be a bit easier as time went on; we eventually got a hand pump outside our house.

Dad heated our house with a cook stove. We did not have all the luxuries that everyone has today (cars, skidoos, riding lawn mowers, four wheelers, etc.). In the winter time when our parents went to town, my dad would take the sleigh and skate back home with all the groceries. Everyone was happy and friendly towards each other. We would borrow sugar, butter, and milk off our neighbours.

We always played in the bush. My father made us a vine from trees, which we could swing from. It was lots of fun. All our friends would come and play with us. We would make forts in the bush. We were poor, but we were happy. I remember mom making a big plate of bologna sandwiches for supper. There was lots of fish suppers too! Families used to visit one another. There was a time when us kids used to go to every household and wish everyone Merry Christmas and the community would give us candies. We would start from one end of the Island to the other. We sure would have a lot when we were finished. The same at New Year's, all of us would wish everyone a Happy New Year, too.

Dave Trumble and Clayton Charles

When I was little, we went to Uncle Ross Peter's house to wish him a Merry Christmas. I was so scared of him that I said my words wrong; I said "Merry New Year and Happy Christmas." All the kids went running out of the house laughing. He was always grouchy. So I guess he scared me. He used to cut my brothers' hair. He would make them sit still. They wouldn't even flinch. I guess they were scared of him just as much as I was.

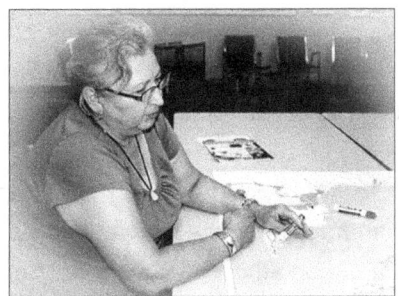

Freda Trumble

Charity, Farmer, Freda and Aaron

In the winter the snow used to be so deep that it would be just as high as the hydro lines. The snow was so deep, our father had to take us to school. We would follow his footprints to get to school.

There was a woman, her name was Edna Porte. She used to make rag mittens for all the children. We used to stop at her house to get warm. She would always give us something to eat and have hot chocolate for us kids. Christmas time was always a happy time. My dad and some of us kids would go into the bush and get our own Christmas tree.

The Island has come a long way. We now have a big school with three classrooms, whereas we only had one classroom. We have a nice Community Centre, Medical Building, Fire Hall, Daycare Centre, Public Works Building, etc.

Long ago our ancestors used to dump all their garbage at the back of their houses. Now we are recycling everything and have a dump that is all in order. We Anishinabe people were told to look after Mother Earth. So in closing, these are a few things that I have seen and learned on Georgina Island. So be kind to one another, love your neighbour and let's all be a happy reservation again.

Meegwetch.

(Freda Trumble, "Life and Times on Georgina Island," *The Georgina Island Storytelling Project*)

Our Summer Cabin
Susan Hoeg tells this story of her family's summer cabin:

Our one room was only thirty feet from our kitchen door. The long summer nights were spent listening to the croaking of frogs and now and then an owl would hoot. Across the lake a faint sound of a train's whistle could be heard. On hot summer nights the cabin brought relief from the heat in our upstairs bedroom.

[In our winter home], as the coal oil lamp flickered, I'd imagine different animals from the shadows it cast on the walls. My grandmother would read her Bible until the oil in the lamp was almost gone. She'd turn down the wick on the oil lamp and cup her wrinkled hand over the top of the lamp glass and gently blow out the flame.

Mom's patchwork quilts kept us warm. She sewed them by hand from old clothes that had worn out. I loved to find a square on the quilt that had been a favourite dress. I loved to listen to the rain on the roof. Sometimes we'd be drifting off to sleep, when we'd hear a mosquito. We'd roll up some newspaper and, jumping all over the bed, we'd try to kill the pest.

An antique double bed took up nearly half the room. At the other end were my grandfather's workbench, a box stove and all his tools neatly hung on the wall. There was a big trunk filled with out-of-season clothes. As each season changed, we'd dig into the trunk finding favourite clothes from the year before. My grandfather hung a quilting frame from the ceiling and there my gran would sew her quilts with beautiful hand sewing. In a corner there was a crock all covered with quilts. Inside I'd love to smell her sweet dandelion wine.

My favourite pastime was to cut out. Expired catalogues were the best. Then I'd put them carefully into an empty chocolate box on a flat 50 tin box. We even had a record player we'd wind up by turning a handle on the side. I loved to listen to old 78 records and sometimes on a battery-operated radio I would listen to the Grand Ol' Opry.

All too soon the summer would end and we'd have to move back into our old log house for another winter. (Susan Hoeg, *The Georgina Island Storytelling Project*, 2006, p. 32)

Getting Modern Services to the Islands
Faith Big Canoe tells this story about postal service on Georgina Island:

This is a story my Grandpa told me.

Way back in the early 1900s, Chief Charles Big Canoe decided to try to get a Post Office here on the Island. He was living in the old house, the big white one (which used to be between Greer and Andy's), of which he had decided to make an office space. He proceeded to enclose an area in the house as soon as you walked in with a desk and drawers and a little window to hand the mail through. They then granted him the right to start the post office over here.

My papa's grandma, Mary-Anne Big Canoe, remembers him going around coaxing people here to write lots of letters to up the volume of the mail so that they would keep the post office running. Once it was established, he would take the Island mail to the Sutton Post Office and bring back any mail for the Islanders. My great-great-great grandfather had to do this every Tuesday and Friday, otherwise they would close it. My great-great grandfather, Charlie, ran the post office for many years afterwards, then his son Albert Big Canoe, and then at last his son who was Lorenzo.

My papa says that he remembers taking the mail to town himself when he was about twelve years old. He said his dad had gotten a boat called a Dispro, which was an inboard motorboat. They would go to the landing in front of the old house where there used to be a big dock and boat-house right up the Black River to just below the Dam, and whoever was doing the mail run would then have to walk to the Post Office on Main Street. During the winter my great grandfather would take the horse sled to town. During the Second World War many of the wives whose husbands were serving overseas would go with the mail boat to shop for groceries and other needed things.

I believe that this in itself has helped us adapt to Island life. We go over for our groceries as we did back then, and we still get our mail through the post office on Main Street though the process has long since [been] updated and [is] more independent. (*Georgina Island Storytelling Project*, 2006, p. 40)

Electrical Power Comes to Georgina Island

After the laying of about two miles of submarine cable and the stringing of about two and a half miles of distribution line on the island itself, electrical power came to Georgina Island on January 16, 1959. This was two years behind the closer-to-the-mainland Snake Island, which first had power in 1957. George Douglas Charles was involved with the process of bringing the power to Georgina Island. He was the first Indigenous person to be a manager at Ontario Hydro.

It was the last community in southern Ontario to have access to electricity. At the official ceremony marking this change on island life, it was declared in the Anishinaabe language: *Wah-Sko-Nah-Sa*, that is, 'the light came on.'

It was hard work putting the poles in. According to Elder Albert Big Canoe, the holes for the poles were dug by hand with shovels and crowbars, and not with fancy pole diggers or other such machines. With the hard yellow island clay and the many rocks, it might take one whole day for a hard-working man to dig a hydro pole hole of at least three feet in depth.

Of course, when some people living on the mainland heard about the "Indians" getting hydroelectric power, they responded with stereotypes, as Elder Albert Big Canoe reported: "I know this is a terrible tale, but I had friends in Pefferlaw and in 1959 when they were putting in the hydro up here, they heard people say, 'What do they need hydro for? What do the Indians need hydro for?' "

Telephone service also came to the island in the 1950s. An underwater cable was laid to connect Georgina Island to the mainland. Initially there was just one phone, at the home of the Big Canoes, because they had the post office. Later, people subscribing to service from a small phone company based in Pefferlaw (before Bell bought all the little companies out) would be put on what was called a "party line." You wouldn't just pick up the phone if you

heard it ringing. You knew that a call was for you (or for someone else) by the sequence of long and short rings. Harold McCue (nicknamed "Scobe"), a man with a sharp wit, would say that his number was 002 short.

Not everyone thought that being connected by phone was an example of much-desired progress. In Elaine McCue's story about her mother, we see that. We also can see that on a party line, you can pick up the phone and hear someone else's conversation:

> She disliked most progress and always said that the old ways were better. When telephone cable lines were laid under the water to our island in 1949, we had a phone installed in her log cabin. We thought she'd enjoy talking to her old friends, the ones that were left, but it wasn't to be.
>
> "If I want to talk to someone, I want to talk to a human face, not a box hung on my wall," she retorted.
>
> This is what our first phones were, a wooden box with a black mouthpiece shaped like a daffodil sticking out of it and a long handle attached with a cable which you held to your ear. There was a small crank on the side of the box; when it would ring everyone could listen on the phone, which they usually did. That way you knew everyone's business and what was going on in their lives.
>
> When I did call my mother, I would have to let it ring and ring, hoping she would get tired of the noise and eventually pick it up. She would respond with a quiet "hello" and only answer questions with a "yes" or "no." I think that she was embarrassed talking to a box on the wall. There was never a goodbye and often I found that I had been talking to a dead phone for ten minutes, not realizing that she had hung

up after the third or fourth question was answered. Then I was the one feeling embarrassed. She never would say goodbye. (*The Georgina Island Storytelling Project*, 2006, p. 6)

Television came to the island a little before electricity. How could that happen? Elder Albert Big Canoe tells the story of having the first television set on the island:

But in the early '50s there was no hydro. My dad got a television set and he got a little Delco generator, put it outside and ran a wire into the house. It had the smallest gas tank, I swear. And we'd be watching television and all of a sudden the machine would quit. Run out of gas.

We used to take the television up to the hall, because the hall had a Delco set. A big one. Every time we went to Christmas concerts and everything we had electric lights because they had a big Delco in the back of the hall. Behind the school actually. Which isn't there anymore. The old school. Where the office is now.

People came and watched. Usually there would be something social going on and then after the social was over, we'd turn the TV on. You'd only get Barrie. And one channel, in Toronto. (*Georgina Island Storytelling Project*)

With those channels you could watch *Hockey Night in Canada* on CBC as well as American shows such as the classic police drama *Dragnet*, starring Jack Webb.

Indoor Plumbing and Washing Machines

Indoor plumbing did not come to the island until the 1960s. That means, among other things, that a lot of people living today who grew up on the island had to use an outhouse when they were young, a major challenge in the winter during the middle of the night. Drinking water had to be brought in from outside sources, streams and the lake, which were still clean enough to drink from.

When band member Mavis Trivett was young, a lot of people did not have washing machines, and used natural soaps rather than the detergents that would harm the water:

A lot of people didn't have washing machines. We'd go down to the lake. You'd pack a lunch, whatever you had. You'd go down to the lake. You'd wash on the rocks. You'd lay them down on the rocks. And that was a whole day, that was a whole day's activity, was to go down and do your laundry at the lake. (*Georgina Island Storytelling Project*)

Changes in the Environment

Major change on the island came with the deterioration of the environment, especially the water in Lake Simcoe. Elder Albert Big Canoe attests to this: "The water was nice and clean when I was a kid. We drank it. It was nothing for my dad going over, to take a cup and have a drink out of the lake."

The accompanying picture provides visual evidence for what he was talking about.

Right: Young Albert Big Canoe Drinking Water from a Pail

Barbara McDonald tells a similar story:

When I was a little girl I used to remember the smell of the lake, of Lake Simcoe. It had a distinct smell. It was fresh. And you could just tell it was fresh. And years ago they used to say Lake Simcoe enabled itself to refresh itself every 24 hours. And that's how I remember it, the freshness and the sweetness of the water when you drank it. Because we drank from the lake, when I was a little girl. Keep in mind that I have been here for three quarters of a century. And I'll be adding one more year on in another week. So I'll be 76 years old.

Oh, the island was just more green, more lush. And it was just absolutely beautiful. And you would even smell the different grasses after it rained. You would smell the sweetgrass coming up. It was just delightful.

You would even smell the mud if you can believe that. The smell of the earth, the sweet smell of the earth. And you could walk in it. And when you were walking along the road, little brown toads used to just jump right out on the road. I don't see those anymore: little wee brown toads. When we were kids we used to pick them up and play with them. We wouldn't harm them; we would just put them back. Actually they were so small that some of them were used for bait when people went fishing. I never saw that, but I knew they were used as bait. They were so cute. I would want to keep a basket of them.

There were more apple trees. And when they would blossom, it would just be gorgeous. It would be absolutely pungent with the smell. It was unbelievable. Now, after all these years the smell is gone. You kind of smell maybe the different gases that are in the air. And I know that some of the rain that falls now harms our trees. Our trees have a funny bark, sort of green and they look scarred. But after a good rainfall, there is some nice smell, but not like the way it was when I was a girl.

Making Their Own Fun

Without television, computers, or cell phones, today's elders had lots of ways of making their own fun when they were children. They certainly feel that they were not doing without anything when it came to fun.

A game often played by school children on Georgina Island into perhaps the 1950s was "Auntie (Ante) I Over." It involved two teams, a soft ball (say one made out of felt or sponge), and a building (such as the schoolhouse) that children could throw the ball over without seeing the people on the other side. Someone would throw the ball from one side, calling out "Auntie I Over," and if no one on the other side caught it, they would yell back the same, and throw the ball over the building. If someone caught the ball, that person would run around to the other side and try to hit someone of the opposing side with the ball (that is why the ball should be very soft). If someone got hit, that person would go to the other side. The ultimate object of the game was to have one side get all the players.

This game was not unique to Georgina Island, but was played elsewhere in North America, including the reservation of the Tulalip people in the state of Washington. It was documented as being played in the nineteenth century. The origin of the peculiar name is something of a mystery. It doesn't come from an Anishinaabe word.

Albert Big Canoe tells of pie socials: "All the ladies would take a pie up and the men and the young men would all bid on it. And if they really liked a pie, they would all pool their money together, bid on this one pie. Then they had to sit and eat the pie with the person who they purchased it from. It was called a social. It was a social gathering, I guess."

"Indian Humour"

As in many a First Nation, adversity, difficult times were dealt with by using humour. Indian agents were white men who exercised tremendous authority over the people from the 1870s to the 1960s. They held the power to tell people when they could go or could not go to the mainland, when and where they could cut wood, and many other decisions non-Indigenous people took more or less for granted.

This would not make these powerful people immune from Indigenous humour. When an Indian agent from Virginia Beach, Wesley Lyons, was appointed in 1940, people would talk jokingly about him by referring to him in their language by the name *mishi beshi*, 'big cat' or 'lion.' Sometimes they would call him "big wind," no doubt because he had a lot of one-sided conversations with them, not because he was adopted by the Georgina family with that last name. The people had little capacity to counter his federal government–mandated control, but they had their humour to get the last laugh on the powerful outsider.

And it wasn't just Indians agents that got their dose of Indian humour. Elders such as Andrew and Albert Big Canoe and Barbara McDonald tell the story of the two Ashquabe brothers, Duncan and Stanley, who, sometime in the late 1940s or early 1950s, were in a small motorboat travelling between the island and the mainland. They lived on Snake Island. The police, who were in a much bigger boat with a significantly more powerful engine, suspected the two brothers had been drinking, then illegal for people who were status Indians. They gave chase.

While the police in their boat had the advantage of being able to travel faster, the brothers could turn to the left or right more quickly, sharply shifting in one direction or the other when the police got close. And they knew the waters well, much better than the police did. Reportedly, the pursuit went on and on for hours. Georgina Islanders saw what was going on, gathered on the shores of the island, and would cheer loudly every time the brothers outmaneuvered the police. Repeatedly cheers were heard across the water. But eventually the motor powering the brothers' boat ran out of gas. They were out of luck.

When the police caught up with them, an officer is reported to have said

"One of you will have to go to jail." Not missing a chance to have the last word, one of the brothers said to the other, "You go to jail this time. I went the last time."

The Language of the Chippewas of Georgina Island

Ahneen, Boozhoo ('Hello'), *Biindigen* ('Come in')—welcome to the section on language. Part of growing up on Georgina Island from the first days to the present is the language. The language of the people, *Anishinaabemowin*, belongs to the family known as Algonquian, the largest Indigenous language family in North America. It has linguistic relatives in every province in Canada, from Mi'kmaq, Maliseet, Innu, Attikamek, and Abenaki in the Atlantic provinces and Quebec, to Ojibwa (under the outsider-imposed names of Algonquin, Mississauga, Chippewa and Saulteaux[34]) and Cree, both of which have communities with speakers in Quebec, Ontario, the Prairies provinces, and even British Columbia. Then there are the Blackfoot languages of Piegan, Kainai (Blood) and Siksika (Blackfoot) in Alberta. Algonquian placenames cover the map of Canada in every province except Prince Edward Island. They include the provincial names of Quebec, Manitoba and Saskatchewan, at least one town in Newfoundland and Labrador, Nova Scotia, and New Brunswick, and the major cities of Mississauga, Oshawa, Ottawa, Saskatoon, and Winnipeg.

There has never been a time in which there weren't fluent speakers of the Ojibwa language or *Anishinaabemowin* in the community of Georgina Island. And now, after decades of decline, more children and adults are learning it. Young adults are studying to become teachers of the language. *Anishinaabemowin* has a future on Georgina Island, and more broadly in many parts of Canada.

The name of the island itself, Georgina, is the feminine version of George (after King George). But Anishinaabemowin speakers still call it *Wasaabigamig* or 'Shining Waters.' All you have to do is look out from the shores of the island on a sunny day to see how appropriate that name is. And Lake Simcoe, named, of course, after Governor John Graves Simcoe, is called *Zhooniyang-zaaga'in* 'Of the Silver Lake.' The first part of the name refers to 'silver' or 'money.' Both *Anishinaabemowin* names tell you something about what the lake looked like in the old days, how it shone. The

---

34. This name is based on the French word 'sault' meaning rapids. This Anishinaabe people had spent time in the area of Sault Ste. Marie.

people are leaders in a number of ways in preserving the quality of the water in Lake Simcoe. They want it to stay clean and keep on shining.

A Good Language for Discussion

In 1957, the issue of parts of Snake Island being "surrendered for sale" by cottagers was addressed by the people and by governments at several levels. Chief John Charles began the community discussion by calling upon Elder Tom Big Canoe to initiate the people's presentation. According to the reporter of the paper that covered the meeting: "He [Tom Big Canoe] felt he could talk better in Indian [*Anishinaabemowin*] than in English because in Indian there was more time for palaver. (The word 'palaver' can refer to a great deal of talking, idle talking, misleading conversation between people from different cultures, and trying to persuade someone.)

Barb McDonald had this to say about growing up with the language: "My mother spoke it fluently [Ojibwe] and she would have spoken it, when I would be in the womb and as I grew up, all my uncles, my grandparents—it was just always spoken. So I never lost it. My whole life. In all my 80 years I never lost my language. But you know, it was tough because of the suppression that they put on us."

Humour with the Language

There is a kind of humour that is unique to the language. When asked whether her mother did quillwork, Barb McDonald responded: "Ya. She used to sit with a bunch of quills in her mouth and I always used to think, 'Haah! What would happen if she inhaled?' Porcupine is *gaag*. I often use that when I speak and I just say, 'Oh my *gaag*.'" Spending time with other elders gives Barb a great opportunity for more humour with the language:

> And people that know me, I like to add in a certain little humour when I talk, like I did today (at the lunch). All the elders, we were sitting in a group. They kept saying, "*Awenesh a'aw*?" And that's such a simple little word. *Awenesh a'aw*. Who's that? Who's that? And it's cute. It's not offensive. You know. "*Awenesh a'aw*." And, I really didn't know anybody myself except my own group. So that's why I explained to the whole group of people because they must have heard us laughing and giggling. Every time somebody came in, we'd say, "*Awenesh a'aw*?" We were being nosy. "*Awenesh a'aw*." All the intonation. I

can say, "*Awenesh a'aw*"—"Who the heck is that?" You know? And I can say, "*Oh—Awenesh a'aw*." That's the way our language works.

The Importance of Hearing the Language Spoken

Hearing the language spoken today does wonders for elders who hadn't heard the language for a while, as this commentary from Barb McDonald shows:

> You know, after I said that prayer today, a woman came over and talked to me and she actually put her arms around me and she was hugging me and she said, "Oh, you don't know what you did for me." She said, "You just reminded me of my gran." She said, "My gran spoke that." She was in tears. And I thought, Oh. I said, "I'm glad to do it for you," and I answered her in our language. And over and over again, she thanked me. See how touching it is to other people? To my people? That somebody else can still speak it?

One of the most important uses of the language in the past, and today is for giving people their "Indian name," as this story told by Elaine McCue shows:

> Years ago it was the custom for our people to give young children their Indian name. This name was usually given to the child by a grandparent or Elder of the tribe at a coming out ceremony in front of all the people. The name usually had to do with a trait or some occurrence within the child's life, usually observed by members of the tribe or a relative.
>
> I have given names when asked to many of my great grandchildren already, and when approached by my granddaughter to give her oldest son his name for the coming ceremony I had to ponder over this situation many hours.
>
> This particular grandchild did not live on the reserve, but always enjoyed coming to spend holidays with his grandmother who did. She was referred to as granny, and I was called *Nokomis* ('my grandmother'), which is my Indian name to him.
>
> Wyatt was about six years old when the naming ceremony was coming up and I had to come up with an appropriate name for him.

Wyatt is a very tall, skinny boy (takes after his father who is over six feet tall) who loves nature and was always inquisitive about all nature and creatures both great and small. His granny lived very close to the lakeshore, and Wyatt loved to go exploring by himself. Along the shore were the marshes and he loved to observe all the different kinds of wildlife he could find.

One day while visiting my daughter, we were sitting outside enjoying the sunshine and keeping an eye on her little grandson. We observe a large crane come landing on the shore at a point where the marsh juts out into the water. Wyatt had also seen this beautiful, graceful bird land there. Neither my daughter or I spoke, but just sat still and watched as Wyatt silently crept closer to the bird which stood very still watching him intently. Wyatt came as close to him as possible. They stood there observing each other silently, then the large crane made a move. He lifted one leg high up to his body, and as he did that, so did Wyatt with one of his long legs. They stood gazing at each other for some time, each one waiting for the other to make a move, as if this was a contest of who could stand on one leg the longest. Then it happened, with a loud "Gwack" the large bird flew silently up in the air.

We watched as Wyatt came running home to tell us of this adventure. "Granny *Nokomis*! That big bird spoke to me!" It was then I had my answer for the naming ceremony.

Wyatt's native name is *Shagi* (pronounced 'shaugie'), which is the name our people gave this beautiful long-legged bird [the great blue heron]. Wyatt was very happy with his new name. (Elaine McCue, "The Naming," *Georgina Island Storytelling Project*, 2006, p. 47)

What Is the State of the Language Today?

In 2021, Statistics Canada found that five people in the community reported that they were speakers of *Anishinaabemowin*. What needs to be mentioned here is that in other federal government reports on Indigenous languages spoken in a community, a crucial three-way distinction is made: fluent-speakers, semi-fluent speakers, and those who report that they are learning the language. The number five most probably reflects those elders who were raised with the language (another number that is sometimes mentioned in government reports), and have spoken it all of their lives. People who are semi-fluent in or learning the language are unlikely to say that they are speakers, even though they may often speak the language.

The Waabgon Gamig school on the reserve reports that it "prioritizes" the learning of the language. On the Culture and Language website, the following statement about language is given.

> It is important to start with the fact that *Anishinaabemowin* faces extinction. The effects of colonization, the residential and mission school system, and the child welfare system in Canada have been devastating to our language, and in turn our People and identity. Our language and culture were originally passed on orally by our Elders and older family relations to the younger generations. This has now changed. Anishinaabemowin now relies on the younger generations to learn and pass on our language to future generations. This preservation of our traditional language is vital as it directly correlates to increased self-esteem and community well-being, and the survival of Anishinaabe culture and identity. Cultural protocols and understanding of the world around us and our place within it are built into our language and the land.
>
> Our Youth are so important in Anishinaabe revitalization, and we hope these links and resources help light the fire of learning in our membership!

This is not just wishful thinking. Those wanting to learn the language are presented with a series of sources that they can access online. These include, among other sources, a dictionary, "Talking in the Kitchen Language Video," "Rochelle Allan—Ojibwe immersion for Families," "Ojibwe immersion story telling by Barbara Nolan" and "Early Childhood Ojibwe Language Resources" (https://georginaisland.com/culture-language).

CHAPTER ELEVEN

Medicines and Medicine People

The word for 'medicine' in Georgina *Anishinaabemowin* is 'mushkiiki', which for a long time has been an effective part of their culture. Dr. John Big Canoe is not alone in being a healer of his people.

Mushkiikiwug: *Medicinal Plants*

One contributing factor in the survival of the people on both Snake Island and Georgina Island is their knowledge of *mushkiikiwug*, or medicinal plants. Their knowledge has done more than keep them healthy. Little known today is the fact that the knowledge of the Georgina Island medicine people also contributed to the health of the people living on the mainland. In 1902, for example, the Indian agent of the time, John Yates, wrote in his annual report: "Some old Indians dig ginseng root and burdock, which they sell to druggists" (Yates, 1902, p. 2). Burdock root (*mazaan(ag)*) has been used in traditional medicines around the world for centuries. So it is no surprise that it was part of the Georgina Island medicine kit for a long time.

The people's extensive knowledge of medicines during the late nineteenth and early twentieth centuries was valued by the settlers on the mainland. This is one of those facts about the people that is not well recorded in history books.

Jiisens *(Ginseng)*

In the *Annual Report of the Department of Indian Affairs* for 1890, the Indian Agent, J.R. Stevenson, reported that the Chippewas of Georgina Island made around $1,000 selling the *jiisens* or ginseng that they had harvested in the wild (Stevenson, 1890, p. 14). That would not be for personal profit, but would be used to serve the community.

It should be pointed out that all *mushkiikiwug* are taken from the woods with great respect for the plants and for the earth according to the traditions. Tobacco (*semaa*) would be offered. Barb McDonald makes that point very clear when she says the following about *jiisens*:

Ginseng. It's a medicine and it's used for many purposes. And the person that will show you, and what you want it for will take you in. And it's kind of, I don't know, I think it's a truism that if the atmosphere is not right and you got the mind for it and I won't right away feel it, but the ginseng will hide on you and it won't let you find it and you can be all around it. And I saw that with Uncle Bud [Big Canoe]. He, he knew and he said we're not going to find any today. It turned out that one of us in the group, how do you say it? had feelings that weren't conducive to us finding it and we just didn't find any. But on our way out a little red flower appeared. Bud noticed and he said as we were coming out "I guess eventually we would have found it, but not today." And it was a good area to be found. It depends on the person you know that's looking for it, because a lot of people who came here dug it up for monetary gain. They just pick it to go sell it because it's used for many things. Well I guess one of us went and picked a few and thought "I can go make a couple bucks cause it's quite valued." But that day we did not find it and we both thought we would because he believed in the customs and honoured everything living and we had tobacco but we didn't find it! But I remember a week after Bud, Wanda [Big Canoe] and I went Weeee ... it was in the same spot. And that's a true story ... it will hide on you.

Barbara (Big Canoe) McDonald

When Barbara McDonald was growing up, Georgina Island still provided a rich store of traditional medicines that were widely used in the community:

They used *wiikenh* of course: *wiikenh* (Sweetflag). That was used a lot. It's very popular among the elders. They use it all the time. All the elders use it. It may not be for a specific ailment but it's something that they believe in. And how they interpret it from their elders. It could be chewed, boiled or stewed. It has a very bitter taste and you don't add anything to it at all.

And then they used to use elm, a slippery elm, *wiishgo*. You would chew that to clear your chest and your throat, it was called slippery elm. Of course they used goose grease for your aches. They even used to rub your chest with goose grease, short of putting us in the oven.

Of course, we used catnip.[35] They gave that to babies so they could sleep good, and to help their digestive system.

And of course we used cedar tea. Cedar tea was used just as a nice social drink. And to help your digestive system, to settle your tummy, it was excellent, cedar tea.

And I used to be amazed at what they used to come up with, what they would make. When we would go to the sugar bush with old Wellington Charles. He would boil the sap, and he'd put something else in it, and that was our drink with our meal... And he would just walk in a little bit further and he would spot it and he would know. And he would just stick it in with the sap. And it would be boiling, and we would all have a cup. It was marvellous.

In a 1960 article in the *Newmarket Era and Express*, Chief Lorenzo Big Canoe spoke of people of Georgina Island with medicine knowledge:

[T]hey did discover some healing qualities with some of the roots and herbs with which they worked marvellous cures.

Some of these remedies are still used by some of us today. For instance, a certain large-leafed plant makes an excellent poultice. There is also a brew of cedar sprigs, slippery elm and chokecherry bark my grandfather used to make to cure our coughs. (Big Canoe, 1960)

Zhaashgob *(Slippery Elm Bark)*

In the *Annual Report of the Department of Indian Affairs* for 1899, and regularly during the first years of the 20th century, the Indian agent spoke of the people, particularly the elders, collecting slippery elm bark (*zhaashgob*) and selling it to local pharmacists. Again this was for community survival, not individual profit. And the people on the mainland benefited from the medicinal knowledge of their Georgina Island neighbours.

Rich in such useful elements as vitamin C and beta-carotene, according to Barb McDonald, "You would chew that to clear your chest and your throat." Unfortunately, as of the last few decades *zhaashgob* is almost completely extinct on Georgina Island, a victim of a changing environment.

---

35. A plant native to Eurasia that was adopted by some Indigenous people and used to good effect.

Wiikenh *(American Sweetflag)*

As mentioned by Barb McDonald, another important medicine long used on the island is *wiikenh* (plural *wiikenyag*; American sweetflag), which was used for a number of different ailments. It grows on the margins of streams and ponds, and can be found as far north as James Bay, so the people would long have known about its capacity for healing long before they came to Lake Simcoe.

Wiingashk *(Sweetgrass)*

Susan Hoeg tells of picking, cleaning, and drying sweetgrass:

> Summer brings special days when I take time to pick sweet grass. Sweet grass is a sacred grass that grows tall with a reddish base and a wonderful smell. It grows in fields and at the forest's edge. If it is cleaned and dried it will last for years. I pick it near the base. After I have a nice sized bundle, I head for home to hours of cleaning.
>
> The cleaning is done by running your thumb or finger down the grass, cleaning any dry pieces off and separating the blades of grass. The grass is then spread out on paper or hung in bundles to dry. At this stage it may also be braided into all sizes of braids.
>
> I use sweet grass when I make hairpieces, wall hangings, place mats and for trimming. I also like to hang bunches in different parts of the house and in my car just for the smell.
>
> Sweet grass is used as a special offering to our Mother Earth and in circles when we pray. We also use it to smudge. Smudging is done by lighting the end of the braid, and putting out the flame so that it only smokes. The smoke is then rubbed onto the body to get rid of negative thinking and bad feelings. It is used for purification, to cleanse both physically and spiritually.
>
> These ceremonies were lost for my generation. They are not being taught to our children by our grandparents. (*The Georgina Island Storytelling Project*, 2006, p. 46)

Medicine Women
Aunt Maggie Jack

One aspect of growing up in Georgina Island in decades past was being raised with the traditional stories of the Anishinaabe people, stories which

A People of Stories

Women gathering and cleaning sweetgrass

could be funny or serious and sometimes quite scary. One of those stories is about shamans that can bear-walk.[36] These are shamans who shape-shift into bears at night. The following story comes from Andrew Big Canoe, concerning his Aunt Maggie. She was wise and knowledgeable in the ways of traditional medicines, and was greatly respected for that reason. She wanted to teach Andrew and Albert Big Canoe about medicines, but they did not show any real interest in it when she approached them, so much of her valuable knowledge was lost when she died in 1968.

Andrew Big Canoe describes her in the following way: "My Aunt Maggie was probably the last medicine person on this island. She knew every herb, every medicine, every plant. If you went back there she'd give you something if you were sick. She'd make you a tea for different types of thing, things for laxatives, things for your kidneys, things for your liver, heart medicine" (2014).

A strong and independent woman, Maggie Jack lived on her own in a backwoods area of Georgina Island, and had done so for decades after her husband died in 1929. So she was a natural subject for rumours to spread. Here is one of those stories.

There was a band of boys gathered around a fire one night, a natural enough situation for trouble to start. It was said that a bear approached the campfire, scaring the boys. They defended themselves by throwing stones at it, hitting it, and eventually driving the bear away.

[36]. A good educational graphic novel that teaches students about these stories as well as entertains is *Adventures of Rabbit and Bear Paws: Bear Walker* by Christopher Meyer and Chad Solomon (Little Spirit Bear Productions, 2011).

The next day it was said that Aunt Maggie appeared with bruises on her body. When she was asked what happened to her, she replied with "I fell." The boys found this hard to believe, but could not prove that she was wrong.

MABEL PRISCELLA JONES CHARLES: HEALER IN TWO TRADITIONS

Mabel Priscella Jones Charles (1907–1983) was a healer in both mainstream Canadian and Anishinaabe traditions. She was born and raised in the Anishinaabe community of Cape Croker or Nawash, but married George Douglas Charles from Georgina Island, where they would both live. Her family long thought highly of education. Her great-grandfather *Kegedonce* ('Orator') said about this about literacy skills in 1830: "As for myself, I am too old to learn, and if I can only hear my children read, I shall be satisfied with what I hear from them" (quoted in Schmalz, 1991, p. 155).

Her obvious intelligence was shown by her early teaching career. She taught at Cape Croker by Sidney Bay, one of three schools in different parts of that reserve. From September to December 1923, at 16 years of age, she taught nine students from grade one to six, and was paid $155. From January through to June 1924, at ages 16 and 17, she was paid $329.

In 1915, Women's College Hospital in Toronto set up a nursing program. The first Indigenous woman to become a nurse was Charlotte Edith Anderson Monture, a Six Nations Mohawk woman who had graduated from an American school in 1914 because that educational door was closed to Indigenous women in Canada at the time. The four Jones sisters would be pioneers in receiving nursing education in Canada when it was available to Indigenous women at Women's College Hospital. Sister Rose would graduate first, in 1923, Ada May in 1927, Mabel in 1928, and finally Flora Iola in 1932. Charles Kegadonce Jones (1852–1952) strongly encouraged and supported this move on the part of his children. He didn't want them locked into the dead end of residential schools.

Going to nursing school in Toronto was not easy for Mabel and her sisters for several reasons. She would take a horse and wagon to Owen Sound. From there she boarded the train to Toronto, where she would live with other nurses-to-be. While there was no tuition to be paid with money, nor monetary payment for room and board, student nurses such as Mabel and her sisters paid in labour by working the patient wards, and doing so nine hours a day, in addition to a scheduled average of one and half hours a day classroom time and the same in study time. Students could be admitted with only one year of high school, but they were put on probation at first, and had to prove their intelligence and moral character. Mabel had clearly had the qualities that they were looking for.

Two weeks after experiencing the joy of graduation, she received a letter from the Department of Indian Affairs saying that she was no longer legally an "Indian" because of her professional status as a nurse. This did not prove to be a problem, as shortly afterwards she married a status man so she regained her Indian status.[37] She had become engaged to become Mrs. Mabel Charles while still studying at school.

She joined the prestigious Victorian Order of Nurses (VON). She practiced as a public health nurse on Georgina Island for 30 years. At one

Women's College Hospital, Toronto, Class of 1928.
Mabel Jones is fifth from the right.

point she had not left the island for five years. The people needed her there, and she was willing to fulfill that need. She received a 40-year community service award from the VON.

She engaged in multiple-purpose healing on the island. She played a key role as a midwife, using the inner bark of the balsam to cut the umbilical cord. Because of the medicinal qualities of that bark, she did not have to disinfect it. In this and other ways she combined traditional medicines with her main-

---

37. Part of the sexist bias of the federal law of the time was that a man with Indian status would not lose it by marrying a non-status woman, but if a status woman married a non-status man, she would lose her status.

Women's College Hospital, Class of 1928. Mabel Jones is on the right in the front row.

stream training. She did service as a wet nurse, one who breastfeeds and sometimes takes care of another woman's baby, also bearing two of her own children. And if someone was sick, she would be the one to decide whether that person would have to leave the island to go to a mainland doctor. Her knowledge of foods expanded her healing role to that of nutritionist, making sure that when outside foods were rationed by the federal government, they received the healthiest foods they could get. She even cut the hair of some of the boys on the island, with what appears to have been a signature cut with a frontal wave high on the right and low on the left.

Left: Graduation Snapshot—Mabel Jones.

CHAPTER TWELVE

Georgina Island Today

We have presented only a few of the many stories of the Chippewas of Georgina Island. While the numbers of the community have never been high, its presence, both locally and now in Canada as a whole, is considerable.

The Georgina Island band today has 775 members. Most of the band members live off the reserve. In 2022, it was estimated that 280 people lived on the reserve, and official figures for 2021 had the number at 235, 50 of whom were younger than 20 and 90 of whom were 60 or more.

The band owns the three islands of Georgina Island, Snake Island, and Fox Island, all in the southern part of Lake Simcoe. There are about 98 homes on Georgina Island and 200 leasing properties. The first leased property dates from 1954. On Snake Island, there are 227 cottage leases. Across the water from Snake Island, near Keswick, is band-owned land. Fox Island has 64 leased properties. The band also owns land on Virginia Beach across the lake directly south of Georgina Island. Newly opened on that land is a restaurant, *Mnookmi* (meaning 'new beginnings'). Even the French toast is made with fry bread or bannock, a real treat not to be missed!

One person largely responsible for these and other innovations in the community is their chief, Donna Big Canoe, the first female chief of the band. She graduated from Georgian College's Indigenous Community and Social Development program in 1998, and was a councillor from 2003 until 2007. That year, at 31, she became chief, and still holds that position as this book goes to press. For further information about her, see Ogimawah Tribal Council, n.d., "Chippewas of Georgina Island First Nation Chief Big-Canoe" at https://www.ogemawahj.on.ca/about-us/board-directors.

The Chippewas of Georgina Island and the Williams Treaties
In early chapters we mentioned the Williams Treaties (named, of course, after Treaty Commissioner Angus S. Williams). They caused hardship for the people of Georgina Island. In 2018, a big change developed in that regard.

Here is the story. During the Williams Treaties discussions of 1923, band members James Asquabe, Charles and John Big Canoe, Benjamin Esquabe,[38] and James Snake (Blair, 2008, pp. 131–2) spoke to the commissioner in favour of recognizing their unsurrendered hunting rights to the northern territories, especially important at the time as there was little hunting left on Georgina Island.

Georgina Island was one of seven Anishinaabe First Nations who signed one of the treaties. The seven First Nations lived in two parts of south-central Ontario. The northernmost three, Chippewas, lived in the area of Lake Simcoe, including the people of Beausoleil, Georgina Island, and Rama. The southernmost four, known as Mississauga, the people of Alderville, Curve Lake, Hiawatha, and Scugog Island, lived much closer to the northern shores of Lake Ontario, and their lands took in much more of the total area of 52,059 square kilometres (12,944,400 acres). There was fundamental agreement over Indigenous land (although much of it was already being lived on, mined, and logged by non-Indigenous people), for which the seven First Nations would receive one-time cash payments. This involved $25 for each band member plus $466,800. Of course, this was far below the actual worth of the land. This was not so much negotiated, but agreed to by the Anishinaabe leaders.

There was significant disagreement, however, when it came to the rights to traditional and much needed hunting, fishing, and plant food and medicine–gathering territories. The Anishinaabe believed that these rights continued, while the Ontario and Canada governments believed that they no longer existed owing to the treaties.

Court cases were to follow to try to settle this disagreement. In 1985, Hiawatha First Nation member George Henry Howard was charged with fishing out of season. When he took this issue to the courts, the Ontario Court of Appeal, it was ruled that the Williams Treaties had extinguished any right to fishing outside of reserves.

This decision was supported in an appeal to the Superior Court of Canada in 1994 which declared, questionably, that the people had knowingly relinquished their hunting and fishing rights in the land surrendered, and that they had no more harvesting rights than other citizens of the province.

This followed the threatening in the fall of 1992 of the legitimate fishing and hunting rights of the Georgina Island people by the Ontario Federation

---

38. The names 'Asquabe' and 'Esquabe' are usually written as 'Ashquabe'.

of Anglers and Hunters (OFAH), who sent a letter to their non-Indigenous neighbours saying that the Georgina community was killing all the fish in Lake Simcoe (Shaule, 2002, p. 13). This was followed the next spring by an ad they placed in *Maclean's* magazine entitled "A Deal is a Deal" in which it was falsely claimed that that they and the Mississauga community had "surrendered their hunting rights for the equivalent of 20 million dollars" (as stated in Shaule, 2002, p. 14).

The federal decision of 1994 was overturned on October 29, 2012, in *Alderville Indian Band et al. v. Her Majesty the Queen et al.* when it was ruled that the 1923 treaty did not involve the surrender of these rights. There were further negotiations until finally in 2018 an agreement was reached. This involved financial compensation of $666 million from the federal government and $444 million by the province, recognition of treaty harvesting rights, and allowing the First Nations involved to add 4,452 hectares to their reserves.

This came with an apology by the federal Minister of Crown-Indigenous Relations, Carolyn Bennett. Unlike what you might expect from a government apology, her presentation reflected an understanding of the difficulties that the people faced because of the government interpretation of the Williams Treaties:

> Unable to freely exercise their treaty harvesting rights, some mothers and fathers were unable to provide for their families as they had before. This, along with other colonial policies and practices, led to hardship and increased dependence on government.
>
> Other members who continued to hunt, fish, trap and gather off reserve or out of season were prosecuted under the law for harvesting. In some cases, these members had their nets, traps, or fishing lines taken from them, while others were fined or imprisoned. Still others were compelled to pursue traditional activities secretively—trapping and catching frogs at night or ice fishing under white blankets—so as not to attract the attention of authorities.
>
> Instead of harvesting being something that family members, both young and old, undertook together with pride, it became a risky activity.
>
> We are sorry that, in not recognizing your rights to harvest in your pre-Confederation treaty areas, your communities faced hardship

and hunger, with the bounties of the land being replaced by biscuits and tins of government meat. We are sorry that your people were not able to pursue traditional activities with pride and dignity, but instead were persecuted for exercising their rights. And we are sorry that your grandmothers and grandfathers, mothers and fathers, and aunts and uncles were constrained in their ability to do what their ancestors had always done—to teach younger generations about your communities' traditional lands and waters and pass along Anishinaabe culture and practices. (Bennett, 2018)

Preserving the Black Ash Heritage

In an earlier chapter we saw how important the black ash tree was in the making of baskets and related items. It also has long provided fuel for heating and cooking. A particular value of the tree in this regard is that it does not need a long period of seasoning as other trees do before it can be used for burning.

Heather Charles

There are on the island approximately 200,000 ash trees which are larger than 9 centimetres in diameter. The Chippewas of Georgina Island are currently quite active in monitoring and protecting the black ash tree on the island, under the leadership of Heather Charles, the Ash Tree Monitoring and Management Coordinator for the band. This involves identifying black ash–dominant stands in which tree planting might be necessary to help maintain the forest cover and keep these wooded areas from becoming treeless wetlands and barren meadows. Such a change would mean loss of forest habitat for species at risk, as well as the loss of shade and its cooling effects for community members, tourists and wildlife. Checking the trees for the invasive and destructive emerald ash borer with detection traps is also part of the band's stewardship of its ash stands.

Fighting for the Water

As they have for so long, the people are fighting for the quality of their water source, Lake Simcoe. This is especially important as they have been under a boiled water alert, like so many First Nations communities in Canada. One such threat came from the Upper York Sewage Solutions project. Owing to the increasing development of the northern part of York County, there is need for the sewage to be treated and released into a body of water. The band council had been told that the treated sewage would be going south to Lake Ontario. But the preferred solution changed, with the treated sewage to be released into the southern part of Lake Simcoe, which would have an impact on life on Georgina Island. Although there is a duty to consult the community, this was not done. The band council found out about the new plans through an article published in a local newspaper. Kerry Charles, the environmental coordinator for the community, met with the deputy minister of the Ontario Ministry of the Environment, the local mayor, the developers, and others to show the band council's strong, unanimous opposition to the idea. On June 20, 2017, the people of Georgina Island also set up a petition directed at the Ontario government, protesting the wastewater plan as well as asking that existing water infrastructure on Georgina Island be rehabilitated and that the site of the abandoned Thane aluminum smelting plant be cleaned up. Before the petition closed, it attracted 35,115 signatures.

In 2022, the concerns of the Georgina Island First Nation were addressed when the provincial government passed the *Supporting Growth and Housing in York and Durham Regions Act, 2022*. It provides for sewage to instead be directed south to a wastewater plant in Durham Region, where it will be treated before being released into Lake Ontario.

Georgina Island: Population Figures in the 21st Century
In the Statistics Canada census profile for the Georgina Island First Nation in 2021, you can read a potentially misleading figure. It states that the number of people is 231. In the same year, the Lands and Management web page gives two numbers concerning the population of the band that reflect a crucial distinction: registered members and those living on their land. The number of registered members of the band is 930, while the number of people living on their land is 208. The latter is the number represented in the government figures. Having most of a band living off reserve is not unusual among First Nations in Canada in the 21st century. The connection is still there. Their ancestors are buried there. Their family members and friends are there.

Bibliography

Allen, R. S. (1995). *His Majesty's Indian allies: British Indian policy in the defence of Canada: 1774–1815*. Toronto: Dundurn Press.

Anderson, J. (1856). *History of Georgina*. LCH Research. ww.lchr.org/a/33/45/History_of_Georgina.html

Anonymous. (2007, July 10). Big Canoe remembered for leadership, volunteer spirit.

Anonymous. (2013, March 7). Buzzy Big Canoe raises $2k. *Georgina Advocate*. https://www.yorkregion.com/life/buzzy-big-canoe-tourney-raises-2k/article_ef0eceb4-5614-5133-88fb-43e389063cb4.html.

Anonymous. (2013, July 17). Buzzy Big Canoe will always be remembered. *Newmarket Era*. https://www.yorkregion.com/opinion/letters-to-the-editor/buzzy-big-canoe-will-always-be-remembered/article_21ac128f-1820-5dfd-b359-1813baac96d9.html.

Anonymous. (2016, October 20). A look at First Nations' prohibition of alcohol. Indigenous Corporate Training Inc. https://www.ictinc.ca/blog/first-nations-prohibition-of-alcohol.

Anonymous. (1949, April 14). Family starving—Indian risks Simcoe ice for food. *Newmarket Era and Express*, p. 1.

Anonymous. (1918). Indian Affairs RG10, volume 2197, file 39, 739-18.

Anonymous. (1865). *North York Intelligencer*, December 8.

Anonymous. (1865). *Newmarket Era*, December 8.

Anonymous. (1938). *Newmarket Era*, September 15, p. 4.

Anonymous. (2013). Our fishing story.

Baldwin, H. (Notetaker). (1846). Minutes of the general council of Indian chiefs and principal men held at Orillia, Lake Simcoe narrows of the proposed removal of the small communities and the establishment of manual labour schools. Canada Gazette Office.

Baraga, F. (1992). *A dictionary of the Ojibway language*. Minnesota Historical Society Press. (Original work published 1850).

Bartleman, J. (2016). *Seasons of hope: Memoirs of Ontario's first Aboriginal lieutenant governor*. Toronto: Dundurn Press.

Bennett, C. (2018, November 17). Statement of apology for the impacts of the 1923 Williams Treaties. Government of Canada. https://www.rcaanc-cirnac.gc.ca/eng/1542393580430/1542393607484.

Benton-Banai, E. (1988). *The Mishomis book: The voice of the Ojibway*. University of Minnesota Press.

Big Canoe, C. (1911). Department of Indian Affairs, RG10 vol. 2838, file 67071-1.

Big Canoe, C. (n.d.). LinkedIn profile. https://ca.linkedin.com/in/christa-big-canoe-219a092b.

Big Canoe, L. (1960, February 11). *Newmarket Era and Express*, p. 8.

Big Canoe, L. (1969). *Newmarket Era and Express*, p. 8.

Blair, P. J. (2008). *Lament for a First Nation: The Williams Treaties of Southern Ontario*. Vancouver: University of British Columbia Press.

Boyle, D. (1898). *Annual archaeological report 1897–8, appendix to the report of the Minister of Education*. Toronto: Warwick Bros. and Rutlen.

Brundle, J. (1952). *The rape of Snake Island*. The Department of Indian Affairs and The Township of North Gwillimbury, Ontario.

Canadian Military Engineers Association. (n.d.). Canadian railway troops: A brief history. https://cmea-agmc.ca/canadian-railway-troops-brief-history.

Charles, R. (1998). Personal journal. https://georginaisland.com/writing/personal-journal-by-richard-charles/.

Cook, W. (1911, February 2). *Orillia Packet*. www.waynecook.com/obits.html.

Copway, G. (1972). *The traditional history and characteristics of the Ojibway Nation*. Toronto: Coles Publishing. (Originally published 1850).

Corbiere, A. (2014). Anishinaabeg in the War of 1812: More than Tecumseh and his Indians. *Active History*. activehistory.ca/2014/anishinaabeg-in-the-war-of1812-more-than-tecumseh-and-his-indians/.

Cruikshank, E. A., & Hunter, A. F. (Eds.). (1932). *Correspondence of the Honourable Peter Russell*, vol. 1. Ontario Historical Society. [statis.torontopubliclibrary.ca/da/pdfs/31385029227608d.pdf].

Dallimore, L. (1984). History of Sandy Cove. *Historical Review of the Innisfil Historical Society*.

Dawson, S. E. (1892). *Sessional papers, volume 10, second session of the seventh Parliament of the Dominion of Canada, session 1892, volume XXV*. Ottawa.

Dunning, R. W. (1974). Some Problems of Reserve Indian Communities: A Case Study. In J. S. Frideres (Ed.), *Canada's Indians: Contemporary conflicts* (pp. 59–85). Toronto: Prentice Hall.

Fleming, E. B. (2017). Nanaboozhoo and the Wiindigoo: An Ojibwe history from colonization to the present. *Tribal College—Journal of American Indian Higher Education*.

Fotheringham, D. (1886*). Sessional papers of the Legislature of the Province of Ontario, volume 2*, pp. 126–127.

Hall, A. J. (2003). Aisance (Aisaince, Ascance, Essens). In *Dictionary of Canadian Biography* (Vol. 7). University of Toronto/Université Laval.

Henry, A. (1809). *Travels and adventures in Canada and the Indian territories between the years 1760 and 1776*. New York: T. Riley.

Hodgins, J. G. (1897). Documentary history of education in Upper Canada from the passing of the constitutional act of 1791 to the close of the Reverend Doctor Ryerson's administration of the education department in 1876, vol. V: 1843–45. Toronto: Warwick Bros & Rutter.

Howes, S., & Atkinson, L. (2013). Charles (Charlie) Warren. Unpublished interview, July 24.

Johnson, T. M. (n.d.). *Georgina Island First Nation: Genealogical and cultural study*.

Jones, H. M. (1960). *Annual report for Indian Affairs*, p. 56.

King, Thomas, (2003). *The truth about stories: A Native narrative*. Toronto: House of Anansi.

Kirk, R. A. (2001). *Hook, line & spear: The ice fishing history of Lake Simcoe*. And So Forth Press.

La Cerise. (1915, October 1).

Leary, T., Marucci, G., McDonald, J., & Williamson, L. (2012, Winter). On the blanket of Mother Earth: First Nations environmental education. *ETFO Voice*.

Lemay, J. (n.d.). *Shingwauk narratives: Sharing residential school history*. Shingwauk Residential School Centre. https://ecampusontario.pressbooks.pub/shingwauknarratives/

MacLaren, Sherill, (1986). *Braehead: Three founding families in nineteenth-century Canada*. Toronto: McClelland and Stewart.

March, W. (2016). RCAF Women's Division. In T. de Bruin (Ed.), *The Canadian Encyclopedia*. Updated 2023.

McCallum, M. J. L. (2008). Labour, modernity and the Canadian state: A history of Aboriginal women and work in the mid-twentieth century (Doctoral dissertation, University of Manitoba).

McCue, Duncan, (2016). *Shoe Boy: A trapline Memoir*. Vancouver: University of British Columbia Press.

McCue, D. (2022). *Decolonizing journalism: A guide to reporting in Indigenous communities*. Oxford University Press.

McCue, H. (n.d.). https://georginaisland.com/writing/going-to-the-church-anniversary-harvey-mccue/.

McDonald, B. (n.d.). Ngoding (At one time).

Meyer, C., & Solomon, C. (2011). *Adventures of Rabbit and Bear Paws: Bear Walker*. Little Spirit Bear Productions.

Miller, J. R. (1996). *Shingwauk's vision: A history of Native residential schools*. Toronto: University of Toronto Press.

Minutes of the General Council on the proposed removal of the smaller communities and the establishment of the manual labour schools (1846). Montreal: Canada Gazette.

Musquakie. (Mayawassino, Waisowindebay) (William Yellowhead). (2003 revision). In *Dictionary of Canadian Biography* (Vol. 7). University of Toronto/Université Laval.

Nation, The. (2014, November 14). Cree doctor wins prestigious Dreamcatcher Foundation Award. www.nationnews.ca/cree-doctor-wins-prestigious-dreamcatcher-foundation-award/.

Need, T. (1838). *Six years in the bush: Extracts from the journal of a settler in Upper Canada, 1832–1838*. London: Simpkin, Marshall and Co.

"Ojibway Indians of Georgina Island in Lake Simcoe; A happy and contented colony of 130 members; Old Chief Big Canoe one of nature's gentlemen, who lives in a well-furnished modern house, and idolizes his grandchildren, just like any white grandfather would do." *Star Weekly*.

Ogimawah Tribal Council. (n.d.). Promoting self-sufficiency among our members; Serving our First Nation communities since 1996. https://www.ogemawahj.on.ca/about-us/board-directors

Pellinger, P. (2014, July 16). Peterbio–Harvey McCue. *Peterborough This Week*.

Riddell, B. (1951). News of the Indians on Georgina Island. *Newmarket Era*. Retrieved from http://archive.org/stream/newmarket_era_and_express_1951_04_05_djvu.txt

Riedner, H. (2014, June 26). Repatriation service part of healing process in Georgina. *Georgina Advocate*.

Riedner, H. (2014, September 20). Community 'hurting' after death of Wanda Big Canoe. *Georgina Advocate*. Updated March 3, 2023.

Schmalz, P. S. (1991). *The Ojibwa of Southern Ontario*. Toronto: University of Toronto Press.

Scott, D. C. (1917). *Annual report of the Department of Indian Affairs*. https://publications.gc.ca/collections/collection_2017/aanc-inac/R1-90-1918-eng.pdf.

Sessional Papers of the Dominion of Canada. (1889). Vol. 22, Issue 13, Part I of the Report of Department of Indian Affairs.

Sgambati, S. (2015, November 8). First Nation Vets remembered—Now it really is all about memory. *Barrie Today*.

Shaule, D. E. (2002). The disputed boundaries of the 1923 (Williams) treaties (Master's thesis, Canadian Studies and Native Studies, Trent University).

Shields, N. D. (2001). Anishinabek political alliance in the post-Confederation period: The Grand General Indian Council of Ontario, 1870–1930 (Master's thesis, Department of History, Queen's University).

Smith, D. B. (1979). Wabakinine (Wabacoming, Wabicanine, Waipykanine). In *Dictionary of Canadian Biography*. University of Toronto and Université Laval.

Smith, D. B. (1985). Jones, Peter. In *Dictionary of Canadian Biography* (Vol. 8). University of Toronto and Université Laval.

Smith, D. B. (2013). *Mississauga portraits: Ojibwe voices from nineteenth-century Canada*. Toronto: University of Toronto Press.

Smith, S. (2008, July/August). Lake Simcoe's own advocate: A Georgina Island anthropology professor has a critical role in forming a lake action plan. *Lake Simcoe Living*, pp. 24–28.

Snake, J. (1846). Minutes of the General Council of Indian Chiefs and Principal Men, held at Orillia, Lake Simcoe Narrows, on the proposed removal of the smaller communities and the establishment of manual labour schools. Montreal: Canada Gazette Office.

Statistics Canada. (2021). Census profile, 2021 Census of Population Profile Table: Chippewas of Georgina First Nation.

Steckley, J. L. (Ed.). (2019). *The memoirs of Alexander Brodie*. Oakville, ON: Rock's Mills Press.

Stevenson, J. R. (1885). *Indian Affairs Annual Report*.

Stevenson, J. R. (1889). *Indian Affairs Annual Report.*

Stevenson, J. R. (1890). *Indian Affairs Annual Report.*

Taylor, S. (2002, July 17). Unpublished interview with Beatrice McCue: Travelling with Quillwork and Baskets.

Turner, G. (2015). *The Toronto carrying place: Rediscovering Toronto's most ancient trail.* Toronto: Dundurn.

Varga, S., Mewa, K., Jalava, J., Jacobsen, C., & Tebby, L. (1998). Preliminary inventory of Georgina, Snake & Fox Islands Chippewa of Georgina Island, July.

Wallace, S. I. (2018, April 11). Williams treaties. *The Canadian Encyclopedia.* Updated on June 24, 2020.

Waubageshig (Harvey McCue M) (1974). *The only good Indian: Essays by Canadian Indians.* Toronto: New Press.

Wesley-Esquimaux, C. (2010). Narrative as experience. *First Peoples Child & Family Review*, 5(2), 53–65.

Wesley-Esquimaux, C. (2021, October 12). First person: Dr. Cynthia Wesley-Esquimaux on truth and reconciliation, historic trauma and the value of mentors. *Alumni and Friends*, University of Toronto Scarborough Campus.

Winegard, T. C. (2012). *For King and Kanata: Canadian Indians and the First World War.* Winnipeg: University of Manitoba Press.

Yates, J. (1902). *Indian Affairs Annual Report.* https://central.bac-lac.gc.ca/.item?id=1902-IAAR-RAAI&op=pdf&app=indianaffairs&lang=eng.

Yates, J. (1907). *Indian Affairs Annual Report.* https://central.bac-lac.gc.ca/.item?id=1907-IAAR-RAAI&op=pdf&app=indianaffairs&lang=eng.

Young, E. R. (1903). *Algonquin Indian tales.* New York: The Abington Press.

Online Resources

http://canadiangreatwarproject.com/searches/soldierDetail.asp?ID=74584

http://central.bac-lac.gc.ca/.item/?id=1883-IAAR-RAAI&op=pdf&app=indianaffairs, Annual Report of the Department of Indian Affairs–1883.

http://georginaisland.com/wp-content/uploads/2014/06/Year-Two-Final-Report-Georgina-Island-April-30th-2014.pdf

http://georginaisland.com/wp-content/uploads/2016/09/COMMUNITY-NEWSLETTER20161-september.pdf____(Georgina Island Updates, September 1, 2016)

http://www.bac-lac.gc.ca/eng/discover/military-heritage/first-world-war/first-world-war-1914-1918-cef/Pages/item.aspx?IdNumber=43105.

http://www.canadiangreatwarproject.com/searches/soldierDetail.asp?ID=74588

http://www.cbc.ca/news/canada/thunder-bay/wesley-esquimaux-named-chair-1.3765579

http://www.fishinglakesimcoe.ca/articles/resources/fisheries-timeline-and-selected-historical-events-of-lake-simcoe.html

http://www.georginaisland.com.php72-37.lan3-1.websitetestlink.com/artifact/birch-bark-canoes-and-teepee/

http://www.veterans.gc.ca/eng/remembrance/memorials/canadian-virtual-war-memorial/detail/2662680

https://elevate.ca/speakers/shelley-mandakwe-charles/

https://georginaisland.com/culture-language

https://georginaisland.com/wp-content/uploads/2014/08/Wil-Wegman-Wild-Rice.pdf

https://publications.gc.ca/collections/collection_2017/aanc-inac/R1-90-1918-eng.pdf)

https://www.ictinc.ca/blog/first-nations-prohibition-of-alcohol

https://www.pressreader.com/canada/toronto-star/20150603/282604556455367

https://www.yorkregion.com/life/buzzy-big-canoe-tourney-raises-2k/article_ef0eceb4-5614-133-88fb-43e389063cb4.html

https://www.yorkregion.com/news/susan-hoeg-awarded-prestigious-order-of-ontario/article_bca411fa-92a0-564d-939a-88e61e9a1b4b.html

https://www.yorkregion.com/opinion/letters-to-the-editor/buzzy-big-canoe-will-always-be-remembered/article_21ac128f-1820-5dfd-b359-1813baac96d9.html?)

The Georgina Island Storytelling Project

Big Canoe, Faith, "About the Mail on Georgina Island," 2006, p. 40.
Big Canoe, Sandra, "Surviving the Trip across Lake Simcoe," 2006, p. 11.
Big Canoe, Sandra, "The Journey Home," 2006, p. 27.
Hoeg, Susan, "A Miracle," 2006, p. 13.
Hoeg, Susan, "Dbaajmowin," 2006, p. 46.
Hoeg, Susan, "Lost on the Lake," 2006, p. 16.
Hoeg, Susan, "Our Summer Cabin," 2006, p. 32.

Hoeg, Susan, "The Island Fire," 2006, p. 15.
McCue, Elaine, "The Naming," 2006, p. 47.
McCue, Elaine, "Telephone." 2006, p. 6.
McCue, Harvey, "Going to the Church Anniversary," 2006.
McDonald, Barbara, "*Ngoding* (At One Time)," 2006.
Porte, Robert, "My New Job," 2006, pp. 19–20.
Porte, Robert, "The Hut Sleeper Sneaker," 2006, p. 43.
Trivett, Mavis, "Before There Were Washing Machines," 2006.
Trumble, Freda, "The Trumbles," 2006.
York, Sam, "The Switch," 2006, p. 8.

www.ingramcontent.com/pod-product-compliance
Lightning Source LLC
Chambersburg PA
CBHW071242070526
44583CB00017B/2302